Praise for *The Weather's Fine*

"In The Weather's Fine, *Arch has declared the truth of his life's work, and more specifically a helpful method for overcoming many of life's challenges. With honest transparency and vulnerability, he shares some gripping personal stories that are difficult to comprehend.*

"If you're going through a battle right now, I encourage you to get this book and learn from his experiences. You'll be glad you did."

- Peter Schweizer, American political consultant and author of the best-selling book, 'Red-Handed: How American Elites Get Rich Helping China Win'

"Families are complicated. Rarely do we get to see inside them. Arch Kennedy takes the reader inside his world. We see the highs and lows of the life of a man not afraid to allow others to learn from his experiences—a truly profound and sensitive book."

- Carol Pocklington, Behavioral Analyst and Author

"I met Arch several years ago when he was in a very dark place. Watching him change his life by incorporating the principles in this book has given me such joy. He is a different man today."

- Amber Goldberg, Atlanta Sales Leader and Personal Mentor to Arch

"Arch's book is heartbreaking, inspirational, and riveting! His openness about his own struggles and challenges gives us valuable lessons that we can all use to be better people."

- Ray Bell, Political Activist, Financial Services Executive - The Wealth Consulting Group

THE
WEATHER'S
FINE

My Method for Navigating Life's Challenges

ARCH KENNEDY

ArchKennedy.com

Readers should be aware that Internet Web sites mentioned as references or sources for further information may have changed or no longer be available since this book was published.

Published by ArchKennedy.com

ISBN (Softcover Trade Edition) 979-8-218-05457-1

Cover design: Heather UpChurch, Art & Design Studios

Interior Art and Layout Design: Heather UpChurch, Art & Design Studios

Editor: Johanna P. Leigh

Trade distribution is provided by IngramSpark. To purchase this book for trade distribution, go to IngramSpark.com or your favorite trade wholesaler.

For media requests and interviews, go to ArchKennedy.com.

Special Sales

Arch Kennedy resources are available at special discounts for bulk purchases for sale promotions or premiums. Special editions, including personalized covers or bookplate inscriptions, excerpts of existing books, and corporate imprints, can be created in large quantities for special needs. For more information, please contact us at Arch@ArchKennedy.com.

Printed in the USA

22 23 24 25 – 10 9 8 7 6 5 4 3 2 1

1st Printing

Dedication

To Leon –
The man who calms the waters.

Contents

Foreword

In the early 90s, I was a morning show host at a local radio station in Dallas, Texas. I remember one of the TV stations announcing a new TV anchor was joining their team. A beautiful woman named Kimberley Kennedy was now on the air in town. I thought it would be a fun radio stunt to profess my love to her on the air and ask her on a date live on the radio. She agreed, and we went on a single date. It was good for publicity, and we had a nice, fun time. But there was no love connection.

Not that long after, I got a job offer and moved to Kimberley's hometown Atlanta, Georgia. She suggested I reach out to her sister Kathleen Kennedy who was also in the television business.

I got to Atlanta, met Kathleen, instantly fell in love, and got shot down faster than I could eat a Chick-fil-A sandwich. But we became good friends after that. She introduced me to her brother, Arch, also in the television business, and I have remained friends with them over the years.

All three of these people were smart, attractive, successful, and just seemed to have everything going for them. It would be easy to be envious of a family like this.

But what you're about to read, confirms that just because someone on the surface appears like they have it all together, most often there's a backstory. Arch Kennedy tells that story in a real, heartfelt, transparent manner that I'm sure was very difficult.

As Christians, it seems like a lot of us are far too quick in our judgment of others. However, it's not our place—that's God's place alone. Those judgments are too often used as a weapon against us by non-believers, in the news, in social media, debates etc.

Being a Christian doesn't mean that we are perfect, or that we have all the answers, or that we do everything the right way. It certainly doesn't mean that we are without sin (only one guy was able to pull that off).

I believe one of the things about being a Christian means we acknowledge that we aren't perfect, but we seek to be better human beings in God's eyes. Those that throw around the spear "hypocrisy" on Christians are usually those who have given up on trying to better themselves. That's sad and doesn't make the world a better place.

Like the rest of us, Arch Kennedy is not a perfect person. In these pages, you can see how he has sinned, grown, repented, and is now spending his life trying to improve on the mistakes he's made in the past. Arch is helping others find the path that he has so thankfully found.

For that, I stand and applaud. I'm proud of you Arch! Keep it up!

I pray we can all continue to grow as well,

Rusty Humphries

Award-winning radio & podcast host of *Celebrating America with Rusty Humphries*

Introduction

What a necessary labor of love and sacrifice this book has been for me because it has two main goals: to help me continue exploring my place and purpose in this world and to offer my life, stories, and lessons learned to help and inspire you.

With those goals in mind, I chose to share my experiences in a topical format instead of chronological order—that is, it's intentionally organized to help you read and apply what I've learned. Some of the intimate and vulnerable experiences I share with you are almost impossible to comprehend, but it is required to fulfill my purpose in writing this book.

You'll also discover very early that the common thread through these challenges and successes is my faith and spiritual journey. As the essence of a spiritual existence should do, it permeates everything—specifically, searching for God's truth for our lives. By digging deep for God's truth in every aspect of my life, I was able to overcome tremendous obstacles, some of which you may be all too familiar with and may be struggling with right now. But hang in there. Whether you've explored the spiritual part of your life or not, it's a vital part of the ongoing restoration process.

When I think back to some of my lowest points, I certainly got there by my own doing. Friedrich Nietzsche, a German philosopher, once said: "But the worst enemy you can meet will always be yourself; you lie in wait for yourself in caverns and forests." Oh, how true that is. I have heard from others all my life that I am too hard on myself. By far, this has been the culprit behind the extreme anxiety and full-throttle addiction I have experienced in the past. Never feeling like I was good enough or feeling worthy of anything good were common emotions that inhibited me from experiencing a life full of contentment.

Would you like to know how to live a life of contentment despite the storms that pummel us along the journey? With God's guidance and wisdom, I'll tell you how I learned that my past pain has not been in vain but can be used for good. When dark, cloudy seasons come, rest assured—God is right there with you.

I'm continuing a path forward that is both fulfilling and (I hope) pleasing to our Creator, and I want you to find that tangible reality of hope and purpose, too. We are not meant to go this road alone, but instead, receive the love of Christ and others. If our lives deviate in some way, we can quickly get back in the saddle. That, to me, is a grace-filled, purposeful life in Christ.

In the moments of the book where I share some very personal, thought-provoking and controversial subject matter, I know I am opening myself up for criticism. If, however, it helps you and others identify and find peace, comfort and wisdom, then it's worth it.

I'll state it plainly that the stories I share are from my personal perspective. My family and others mentioned may see these experiences through a different lens. Despite some very tumultuous times in my family's past, I'm thankful today that I have always had strong relationships with my sister, Kathleen, and my father, Arch Jr. As of this writing, though, I'm waiting on God's restoration with my oldest sister, Kimberley. The events you'll read about put a rift in our relationship so much that we have not spoken in many years. The challenges continue in life, don't they? But I choose to keep hope alive that reconciliation and healing are possible.

Get ready for some rocky moments in this book but know that there is victory on the other side of them.

CHAPTER 1

My Most Important Decision

"God aims first to renew man's darkened spirit by
imparting life to it, because it is this spirit which God
originally designed to receive His life and to commune with
Him. God's intent after that is to work out from the
spirit to permeate man's soul and body."

— Watchman Nee

The most important thing to me is my faith in Jesus Christ, and the love of Christ was ingrained in my being from childhood.

We went to church in my small little Georgia town every Sunday, and I was always dressed in a coat and tie to show respect for our Creator. I'll never forget my little clip-on ties since I was still too young to tie one myself. As many sermons went over my head, Mom would let me draw on my church bulletin to pass the time. I can remember always being excited after church because we would get a trip to McDonald's for lunch.

My parents laid a wonderful foundation for me that I will always be grateful for, and even though I strayed away from church and God in my twenties, that foundation thankfully led me back years later. When I got older, I would hear so many horror stories from other gay people about how bad the church had been to them and why they will never go back. With huge resentment, they would describe how many times they were told they were going to hell for being gay, that God did not love them, and neither did the people in the congregation—nor were they welcome there. It has always saddened me to this day, as I did not have that experience in my younger years. It would not be until fifty-one years old that I would experience my first and only time being actually rejected from a church.[1]

Small Town and Big City Experiences

My little Central Georgia town had a population of about 9,000 people, and you knew everybody, and everybody knew your business. Oddly, after hearing the horror stories from others in the gay community, I never once heard my small town preacher even mention the word homosexuality in his Sunday sermons. I never even heard other friends talk about gay people. When I got older, I lived in several fairly small cities, including Macon, GA, Athens, GA, and Tallahassee, FL. My career also took me to bigger cities like Orlando, Nashville and Atlanta. In each of those cities, I tried a church or two, and in none of those places did I ever hear a preacher say that gay people were going to hell, and I was never made to feel that I was not welcome as a gay man. Granted, I did not vocalize my sexuality, but the topic was never brought up in church sermons nor with other churchgoers.

---

1   archkennedy.com/2021/10/04/what-would-jesus-do

The one account I can remember where homosexuality was mentioned in church was ironically at a very large Presbyterian church in Atlanta. At this time, the Presbyterian church on a national level was divided between a more conservative branch and a more liberal branch. That day the preacher said he did not like to do any politics in church. Still, he had to tell the congregation that this particular Atlanta Presbyterian church was siding with the conservative branch, which did not believe in gay marriage. That was all he said. Still, I heard nothing about gay people going to hell or not being welcome in the congregation, but many gay people on the liberal side would have walked out immediately.

My Faith Is Put to the Test

Growing up in a southern, Christian, conservative family, I was not excited about the thought of telling my family that I was gay. The double life was still going on with respect to my mother, father, and two sisters. Hiding this major aspect of my life grew very tiresome, as I was always having to lie about what I was doing and where I was going. At age twenty-one, I could not take it any longer, and I reached out to my more "open-minded" sister, Kathleen. My oldest sister, Kimberley, was very judgmental and religious in my eyes at the time. Later, I would find out that my fears were validated. The thought of telling her terrified me, but the middle child, my second older sister Kathleen, was a bit more of a free spirit. She had been an acting major and danced in Six Flags shows, so she had often been exposed to quite a few gay men. I knew this and had a sense of security in telling her first. My intuition was correct, and Kathleen kept my dirty little secret from the rest of the family for three years.

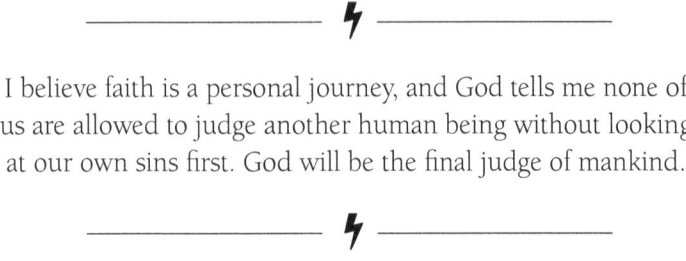

I believe faith is a personal journey, and God tells me none of us are allowed to judge another human being without looking at our own sins first. God will be the final judge of mankind.

This parable from the Gospel of Luke in the Bible is a cornerstone for this statement:

> "Now the tax collectors and sinners were all gathering around to hear Jesus. But the Pharisees and the teachers of the law muttered, 'This man welcomes sinners and eats with them.'

> "Then Jesus told them this parable: 'Suppose one of you has a hundred sheep and loses one of them. Doesn't he leave the ninety-nine in the open country and go after the lost sheep until he finds it? And when he finds it, he joyfully puts it on his shoulders and goes home. Then he calls his friends and neighbors together and says, "Rejoice with me; I have found my lost sheep." I tell you that in the same way there will be more rejoicing in heaven over one sinner who repents than over ninety-nine righteous persons who do not need to repent'" (Luke 15:1-7).

The reason I'm making a clear statement about judging others is because what I am about to say tends to anger people on both sides of the spiritual aisle. Granted, the topic of the sin of homosexuality seems always to get the most spotlight in political discussions, but there are plenty more sins illustrated in the Bible. We are all sinners.

I have battled with my faith and sexuality all of my life and still do today, but I am beginning to develop a hypothesis on why I have had to go through the pain of being gay and a Christian at the same time. I tried for many years to pray the gay away. I did therapy and tried to date girls to be attracted to them—but to no avail. After a decade of fighting it, I finally dealt with the reality that I could not change my same-sex attraction. I pushed it to the back of my mind and tried to live my life as a gay man searching for a healthy monogamous relationship.

I'm reminded of a quote from a former Australian evangelist in the Assemblies of God, Anthony Venn-Brown, that says, "My faith is a choice. My morality is a choice. My sexual orientation however isn't."

My Controversial Conclusions

As my faith and wisdom have grown, I have come to some controversial conclusions depending on one's personal and spiritual worldview. What if my homosexuality is my arthritis? Let me explain. My mother suffered more than any human being I have ever witnessed with severe rheumatoid arthritis. She started having pain in her joints as early as in her twenties, was using a wheelchair by her forties and was bedridden, having to be bathed and fed for the last thirteen years of her life. Anyone who knew her could tell you they have never seen another person suffer as long and hard as my mother.

Despite this, she never lost her faith and had a will to live like no one you have ever met. Her pain was not in vain, as she was an inspiration to many who knew her. What if my homosexuality and alcoholism are my arthritis? In other words, what if I am to use this pain to help others fight these same demons like my mother helped so many with her will to live?

One thing I will not do is change God's word to suit my needs and my sinful nature. There are certainly passages in the Bible that discuss this topic of homosexuality:

> *"Do not have sexual relations with a man as one does with a woman; that is detestable"* (Leviticus 18:22).

> *"If a man has sexual relations with a man as one does with a woman, both of them have done what is detestable. They are to be put to death; their blood will be on their own heads."* (Leviticus 20:13).

> *"In the same way the men also abandoned natural relations with women and were inflamed with lust for one another. Men committed shameful acts with other men, and received in themselves the due penalty for their error"* (Romans 1:27).

> *"Or do you not know that wrongdoers will not inherit the kingdom of God? Do not be deceived: Neither the sexually immoral nor idolaters nor adulterers nor men who have sex with men nor thieves nor the greedy nor drunkards nor slanderers nor swindlers will inherit the kingdom of God"* (1 Corinthians 6:9-10).

> *"We also know that the law is made not for the righteous but for lawbreakers and rebels, the ungodly and sinful, the unholy and irreligious, for those who kill their fathers or mothers, for murderers, for the sexually immoral, for those*

practicing homosexuality, for slave traders and liars and perjurers—and for whatever else is contrary to the sound doctrine" (1 Timothy 1:9-10).

"Now for the matters you wrote about: 'It is good for a man not to have sexual relations with a woman.' But since sexual immorality is occurring, each man should have sexual relations with his own wife, and each woman with her own husband" (1 Corinthians 7:1-2).

I choose to keep this life challenge between God and me and not to make it a political or personal debate with another person.

We are all on our own journey and at different places in our growth as children of God. From the above passages and more, I believe scripture is telling me that God wants me to remain celibate and has put this trial in my life for me to grow closer to Him. I plan to keep reading scripture and searching for God's truth, not mine or anyone else's. This dichotomy infuriates both the liberal and conservative gay community and even some straight people, too. I understand because the question arises: "Why would a just God produce a child this way and then tell them they are sinners for what they can't control?" Great question. But, then I would ask, "Why did He create a woman like my mother to suffer most of her life with a debilitating disease?"

———————— ϟ ————————

The answer? We are not in heaven.
We are all sinners living in a broken world,
and this is why we need Christ.

———————— ϟ ————————

He died for our sins. What an incredible gift. When I concentrate on this above all else, the sexuality dilemma kind of loses its punch. When I concentrate on Christ, all of my sins lose their punch. In other words, my sins become less and less the closer my relationship grows with Jesus. This has been an evolution that has taken fifty years to come to fruition.

Even though I left God in my twenties, I know God never left me. Alcohol and my sexuality took me away from Him for a decade. I know now that my alcoholism put a block between God and me. I could never have a relationship with Christ while drinking.

When you study addiction, you understand that the drug of choice becomes the most important thing in your life—more than anything else. Once addicted, the brain actually "needs" the drug to feel normal. This is when it is no longer a "choice." The addict is "hooked."

The great news is that while you can't be cured, addiction can be treated with detox and rehabilitation and luckily, I made that positive choice. I attribute finding Christ again later in life to the wonderful early spiritual foundation my loving parents instilled in me—Christian values that were deeply imprinted on my heart and soul. I am thoroughly grateful for that. What is also great news is that you don't have to have that foundation to find Christ at any point in life. He is always waiting for us. We just have to look for Him and have that desire to do so. Another incredible gift.

Spiritual Brokenness in the Gay Community

I came out as a gay man at 18 years old. I found the gay scene and encountered some gay men who were treated very badly by their families and church when coming out. Some actually were abandoned by their family for being gay. Many young men did not have the same experience as me as a child, so I understand the hurt and pain that some have gone through. Luckily, I did not.

But through my twenties, I heard a few different stories from gay men who were told they could never have a relationship with Jesus Christ and were going to hell, and they developed a deep hatred for church and for God. I would find out later that the number of churches spewing this hate and judgment was not nearly as many as the liberal gay population portrayed.

To be quite blunt, there is a huge sense of victim mentality in general with left-leaning people politically, especially with the gay left. It is understandable that one would be hurt and resentful, to an extent. But I never believed that one should wallow in these resentments forever. Also, I was lucky enough to know that these hateful words came from people and not from God. So some gay people are very mad at God. And I get it.

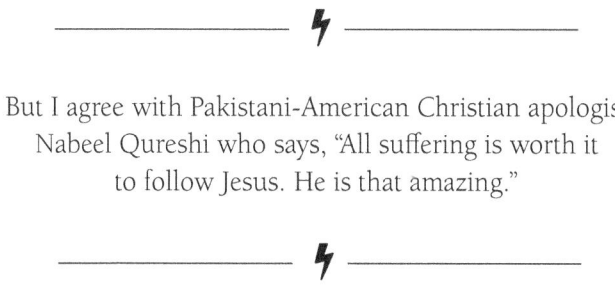

But I agree with Pakistani-American Christian apologist Nabeel Qureshi who says, "All suffering is worth it to follow Jesus. He is that amazing."

My Method for Dealing with This Life Challenge:

Understanding that this type of hatred comes from people and not God Himself is crucial. And everyone is responsible for recognizing and accepting this fact if they ever want to feel the fullness of Christ in their hearts. Will gay people get to heaven? If they accept Jesus Christ as their Savior, yes. But, there is way more to it than that. My pastor said something so simple to me and yet so profound. He said, "Your answers will come from reading Scripture. All of our answers are there. We just have to open our hearts and souls to what God is telling us." In my early fifties, I am finally doing it. I feel completely confident that much more will be revealed as I continue to read the Bible and ask God for an understanding of His truth in every word I read. Today, I am also finding as I read and understand more of God's Word, the more I desire to be more like Christ.

As it stands for me today, I think I will struggle with my sexuality until I develop a deeper relationship with Jesus Christ. Yes, there are various passages in the Bible that reference homosexuality as an un-acceptable practice and an abomination.

How do I cope with this? With constant prayer for God's truth to be revealed to me. It is a personal journey and struggle, and I certainly will never make it political. Right-leaning or left-leaning church pas-tors will undoubtedly have differing opinions on whether one can have a healthy and loving gay relationship with God's approval. What I do know is that my seeking Jesus Christ is the main purpose of my life, and through this, the truth will be revealed to me through reading the Word. And as those truths are revealed, I will have more and more of a desire to do God's will.

Here's the Truth:

Jesus welcomed all to follow Him and told us He is the way to heaven. As long as I continue to pursue Him, I will strive to be more like Him and eventually be with Him when I finally leave this physical body. That gives me comfort and peace.

CHAPTER 2

Coming Out One Step at a Time

"My choices, it seemed, were to be branded a sinner and
live my life alone; to abandon my faith, the one thing I held
most dear in the entire world; or to lie to everyone,
pretend I was straight, and forget about it all."

– Justin Lee

I first discovered I was gay in high school. The self-discovery was
slow, as I was just going through puberty and realizing that I was
a sexual being in the first place. Julie and I sat close on the bus coming home from a football game, and I could tell by her swooning
attention that she liked me. I also felt a lot of pressure from friends
who had already kissed a girl, so it was the dreaded time and place
for me to get it over with. My anxiety was through the roof. She gave
me all the clues about what she wanted, so we kissed. I'll never forget
that first real, open-mouth kiss. It felt very interesting, in fact, kind
of good. But no sparks. I felt I could finally check that off my list of
things I needed to do since everyone else was doing it. But that is all
that it was, a checklist. There was no feeling of wanting to do it again.

As high school went along, my friends started going out on dates as soon as we started driving. All I wanted to do was hang out with my friends. *Why was that*, I thought to myself? I felt different, and I wasn't sure why. One of my best friends was one of our star football players. David[2] was unusual, given that he matured physically much quicker than the rest of us. He had the body of a 25-year-old, although we were only 16 in actual years. We had a great time spending some nights at each other's house like everyone at that age. Watching MTV and horror movies till all hours of the night was a regular thing.

One night, David fell asleep before me. I had an incredible attraction to him, and I just couldn't resist. I reached over and touched him over his clothes, let's just say, in a private area. It woke him up, and I quickly pulled back and acted like I was asleep. I don't think he even realized what I did as he was asleep when it happened. It was at this point that I thought I was gay. I would spend the rest of my high school years suppressing these feelings telling myself that it was just a phase. I would grow out of it.

A Life-Changing Season

The summer between high school and my first year of college was a life-changing time in my life. I had my first physical experience with another man. I had started working out at the gym during high school and was going to the gym daily during that summer, enjoying my last bit of free time before heading off to the University of Georgia. Jeff was about four years older than me and was home for the sum-

---

2   Some fictitious names are changed in the book to protect their privacy.

mer. We started talking at the gym one day and, for the first time, had become actual friends. Jeff had been in a fraternity at Georgia and would tell me all about what I would expect at college. I was very excited. I noticed something different in our friendship that developed that summer. He flirted with me, and I liked it a lot.

At first, I did not know how to handle it and eventually found myself flirting back. We started hanging out, and one night he came over with a twelve-pack of beer. We both became a little buzzed, and I found myself lying with him on the couch. I will never forget just lying there with my arm around his waist. It felt wonderful. Nothing else happened that night, but it was that night that I knew I was gay.

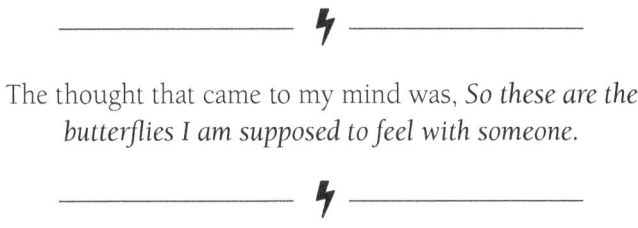

The thought that came to my mind was, *So these are the butterflies I am supposed to feel with someone.*

All the dating my friends did in high school made sense now. I finally understood what they felt with their girlfriends. That summer at age 18, I had my first physical relationship with another man, and it felt incredible. The shame of who I was seemed to melt away... at least for a while.

My College Experiences

Jeff introduced me to his fraternity that fall, and my college life and "double life" began. I was accepted and went through pledgeship growing my friendship with some great guys. Athens only an hour from the major city of Atlanta, and I often found myself on that road. I was, of course, not out at school, so my refuge would be week-end trips to the big city and the gay bars, where I felt totally at home and safe. As expected, as a 19-year-old, the hormones raged, and sexual encounters would become quite frequent. I would feed this need in Atlanta only to return to Athens and pretend to like and date girls. The charade would continue during my first two years of college. Toward the end of my pledgeship, at a New Year's Eve party, the drinks were flowing, and Jeff and I escaped outside for a few minutes. My greatest nightmare had happened. While kissing outside, one of my fraternity brothers came outside and saw us. My heart sank, and I was paralyzed with fear. What were the brothers going to say? What were they going to do? It would not matter because, at this time, I was also flunking out of school. Drinking had overtaken my life, and I was not studying nearly enough. I attribute this to the double life I was living. It was very hard to do. I was also not happy with my major, so I made some tough decisions. I left the University of Georgia and transferred to Florida State University, where I would major in meteorology—something I had been seriously thinking about for a while. It was there I would have what I considered the best three years of my life up to that point.

After the two years of living a lie both at home and at school, I decided to move to Tallahassee to pursue a meteorology degree and that I was not going to be "in the closet". The juggling of straight college friends and gay friends was thoroughly exhausting. Meteorology is a very hard major, requiring a lot of calculus and physics. I worked hard, and I played hard. The "play" consisted of a lot of bars and drinking. I made it a point to always finish my studying before going out on the town.

It's amazing what you can do when you are young. The rebounds from nights out partying were quick, something I could never do now. I can remember the feeling of being free to be myself for the first time in my life. Along with the great times, I was having severe panic attacks on the days after drinking heavily. I remember being in class and several times having to get up and walk out, even during a test. Along with the panic attacks, I would sometimes have a nosebleed which increased the anxiety during the attack. I pushed through those and continued working hard and playing hard. But it was getting harder and harder on my mind and my body.

After three years, I finally received my meteorology degree, and I don't think there was anyone happier than my advisor, Dr. Henry Fuelberg. While he had his doubts about me in the beginning, I felt he was genuinely happy to see me succeed. I will always remember him and be thankful to him for his direction and support through college.

Coming Out to My Family

Having two older sisters in broadcasting, I had a bit of an advantage given that I was able to make a demo reel that would be used in getting my first job. Because my mother was getting severely crippled, I wanted to start my career as close to home as possible. Also, I loved my mother and just wanted to be closer to her in general. I always heard there was no greater love than the love between a mother and a gay son. That held true for me. I think her illness also made us closer than most families. She needed a lot of physical help as far back as I can remember, and it only got worse every year she got older. My sisters and I were so close to Mom and her illness that it made it incredibly difficult to have healthy boundaries, which caused a lot of stress on the family as a whole.

My sisters never wanted me to go into television. They thought the business would eat me alive since I was generally a very sensitive person. The business is very cutthroat and not for the faint of heart. This is probably why I started as a business major at UGA. There was really nothing else I wanted to be but a weatherman.

After graduation, I pulled my little U-Haul with my three pieces of furniture and headed home to Thomaston, Georgia to live with my mother until I could land my first job. Wanting to be close to home, I sent my demo reel to all the small Georgia markets. I will never forget my sisters telling me, "Now be prepared to not find work for a while, possibly up to at least six months." I was working as a weeknight meteorologist the following week in Macon.

My first job paid $16,000 a year. Since I could not afford an apartment, I lived with Mom and commuted to Macon five days a week. Living with my mother was making it increasingly hard to hide my sexuality. More and more, Mom and Kimberley, my oldest sister, were asking me about dating. The stress of my first job on air and the hiding were getting the best of me.

On New Year's Eve 1994, I got home from work just in time to watch the ball drop in New York City with Mom. Tears filled my eyes, and I said, "Mom, I have to tell you something." Her face went pale as I think she knew what I was about to say. They say moms always know. I said, "Mom, I'm gay, and I can't help it."

She started crying, asking, "What did I do wrong to make you this way?" She went straight to blaming herself for my homosexuality, and I knew well in my heart that she had nothing to do with it.

─────────── ⚡ ───────────

That was one of the hardest things I ever had to do. As if her severe illness wasn't enough, I had to add this to her list of problems. But I could not hide it any longer. I knew I could not change—as hard as I tried to pray it away. I could not think of one more excuse as to why I was not dating girls. Kathleen, the more open-minded sister, kept my secret for about three years, so I know this eased her stress not to have to hide it from Kimberley and Mom anymore. Of course, Mom told Kimberley, and I got one of the most hurtful, heartbreaking letters of my life. Kimberley was, at this point, a weekday anchor at the NBC affiliate in Atlanta. The letter came in the mail, and my heart sank as I read it. I knew what it was about, but what was it going to say? I always felt she was extremely judgmental, so it was not going to be good. She was hugely religious, and I believe, has always used it as a weapon. My previous intuition about telling her proved correct.

She expressed how angry and disappointed she was in me. She said, "This is the final straw that will finally tear our family completely apart. How could you do this to Mom?" There was plenty more in the letter that I can't even remember at this point and frankly worked very hard to forget. What hurt so much was that I knew I could not change my same-sex attraction, and I was already in great pain being gay. I could not even accept myself. This letter was salt rubbed into an already deep wound. I kept that letter for years. It would not be until years later into my sobriety that I tore it up and threw it away. Forgiveness sometimes takes a long time. I had one more person to tell, and that was my dad. That would not come until a few years later. Why? My father was a military man and a pilot for Delta, a man's man. I feared telling him most of all.

My Family's "Intervention"

It wasn't long after I told my mom and sister when I got a call to come over to my sister Kimberley's house in Atlanta. At the time, I was still in my first television job in Macon. I would spend my off days in Atlanta going out to gay bars and hanging out with gay people who loved me for who I was. I could be myself there. My family knew I spent my off time in Atlanta—and now they understood why. I had no idea what was going on, and honestly, I can't remember how they asked me. I just remember what happened, as it was a hugely unpleasant experience in my life and one I will never forget.

It was much like an intervention for a drug addict. My two sisters and mother were sitting right in front of me like a panel of judges. They gave me an ultimatum. I could either be straight and leave the gay "lifestyle" or not come home again. My heart sank and a knot developed in my throat as tears welled up. I was not prepared to hear these words, and I knew in my heart that I could not change being attracted to men. So, I guess I did have a choice. I could start a *pretend life* as a *pretend straight man* and have my family, or I could resume my life as a gay man without my family.

The pretending at work was hard enough for me, and I was in a stressful occupation of television news, so I just could not see pretending to be straight for family any longer. I had just come out to them because of the anguish resulting from my secret and the stress of keeping that secret. So I left Kimberley's house crying, unbearably sad that I had just lost my whole family. What was I to do?

Luckily, at the time, I had met a sweet man named John, who showed me kindness and would let me stay at his condo with him and his partner in Atlanta on my off days. He was from a small town in South

Georgia and knew what I was going through with my family as he had a similar family experience. He was about ten years older than me and was a wonderful person to confide in. I will forever be thankful to him for giving me at least some type of family structure when I had just lost my entire family.

About six months went by, and I got a call from Kathleen. She didn't mention a word about what had transpired months earlier and proceeded to tell me about a job opportunity at CNN she had heard about. She was working there as an anchor at this point. She said I needed to get her an audition reel pronto. We chatted a while, and never once did she mention the "gay intervention."

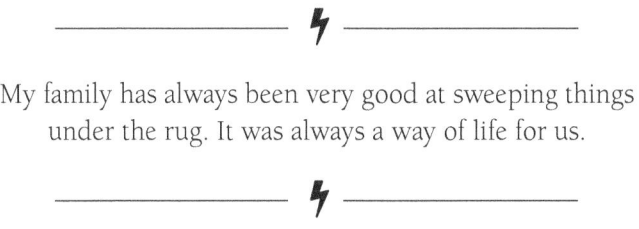

My family has always been very good at sweeping things under the rug. It was always a way of life for us.

They say you only vividly remember impactful moments in your life. I honestly cannot remember how I began talking to Kimberley and Mom again after all of this. It is all very hazy. But eventually, we all just agreed not to talk about my sexuality and dating life. So my double life continued—my work and family where personal things were not discussed and my leisure time with friends where I could be me. It is certainly not an optimum way to live your life, but I made do for a long, long time.

One More "Intervention"

My family did one more "intervention" with me. They decided to take me to a "Christian counselor" to discuss my homosexuality. I remember the day vividly. Kimberley went with me, and we actually went into the session together. I loved my family and would do anything to try to mend our tainted relationship. It started out okay, but then he asked me if I wanted his help to stop being a homosexual. My heart sank. I had already tried to pray the gay away for years, and I knew in my heart I could not change my same-sex attraction. I could choose to be celibate, but I knew I could not change what I was attracted to.

I got very angry and walked out. They tried one more Christian counselor at my sister's church, Peachtree Presbyterian Church in Atlanta. I was willing to go because I loved my family more than anything. I did this session alone, and it went really well. The counselor just talked to me and listened to my struggle with my sexuality and my faith. He told me that I needed to search for God's truth and have long conversations with Him who created me. It didn't really solve my issue, but it really gave me comfort to have someone to just talk to without judging me. When I told my family about my session, my mother and Kimberley said he didn't know what he was talking about and that I should not go to him anymore.

The Relationship Journey

During the next decade of my life leading into sobriety, I dated men but never had a long-term relationship, which I desperately wanted. Even though I had somewhat accepted who I was, I hated being gay, and to this day, I wish I wasn't. I found over the years that men can be very promiscuous if allowed, and most do not want a long-term relationship even when they say they do. If gay men do get into relationships, many open them up to sex with other people.

In over 30 years of being "out", I can count on one hand how many gay men have lasting monogamous relationships. It is my belief that all men are sexual beings, and for straight people, women tend to keep men in check sexually most of the time. When it comes to two men together, there is not a lot of power on either side to refrain from sexual behavior.

Over the next three years, I think God was working in hearts of Mom and Kimberley, as they softened and began to accept the fact that I could not change. I began to be able to discuss my private life a bit more. As time went on, I felt comfortable enough to have the talk with Dad. He was the one I was worried about the most. What would he say? Would he abandon me? I find it funny how we remember pivotal events in life: where we were at, who we were with. Dad and I were getting off the Georgia 400 exit to the Buckhead loop at Lenox mall. I said, "Dad, I have to tell you something. I'm gay."

Well, just when you think you have people and life all figured out, God throws us a curveball. He answered, "Oh son, I knew that and it's ok with me." My jaw dropped. Here I was worried for years to tell my father, and he was the one who took the news the best. Go figure.

———————————— ϟ ————————————

Each disclosure to a family member took a little more stress off of me and made my life a little better.

———————————— ϟ ————————————

My first and only long-term relationship came at the age of 41. Moving home to take care of my mother and to be near loved ones, after about a year of being home, I met Leon. I was doing some volunteer work for Emory Vaccine Center research, and Leon was president of an annual bike ride event to raise money for AIDS research at the center. We had worked out at the same gym, and I recognized him at the ride, and we got to know each other a bit. He was the first gay man I had met that had a good head on his shoulders. You would not have known he was gay if you didn't know him. I never met anyone who had a bad thing to say about him; he was just an all-around good man.

So one day at the gym, we were talking to the manager, who was a good friend of both of ours. She takes pride in that she was the one who introduced us. I love to joke about my pinching his dark skin and hairy legs that day. He is half-Mexican, so the dark skin was a plus for me. Leaving the gym that day, I mustered the courage and asked him out. The rest is history. Ten years later, he is still with me through the hardest decade of my life: the slow loss of my dying mother and my alcoholism which took me in and out of hospitals and rehab for eight years. And by the end of my mother's life, she and both of my sisters, as well as my father, would end up loving Leon like family.

Mom used to say: "Leon is the man that calms the waters." How true that statement is. In our high-strung family, where arguments would get quite heated between my two siblings and me, he could bring the heat down a notch or two. One of many things I am immensely thankful for is that my mother died knowing exactly who I was and loving Leon and me unconditionally.

My Method for Dealing with This Life Challenge:

Even though my coming out story has many similarities to those of other people, it was still very personally unique to me. It was my journey and no one else's. Though I couldn't change my sexuality, I knew that telling my loved ones would be painful. It was never my goal to cause pain, but it happened, nonetheless. There were several pleasant surprises along the way, too. I did it on my timetable, and each opportunity to share a little more of who I was, took away more and more stress from this major life challenge.

Could I have probably done some things better along this journey? Yes, but I still have few regrets, and I know that God loved me through it all. Time has brought some reconciliation and restoration, and I'm grateful for that. It gives me the purpose and strength to help others on a similar journey.

Here's the Truth:

The legitimate truth about one's sexuality can't be ignored, and it's a very personal decision on when and how to discuss it with others. Pray for and receive God's truth, strength, and wisdom as you embark on this journey.

CHAPTER 3

Finding My Work Passion

"Sunshine is delicious, rain is refreshing, wind braces us up, snow is exhilarating; there is really no such thing as bad weather, only different kinds of good weather."

– John Ruskin

I developed a love for weather in high school. Growing up on a farm in the middle of nowhere, I remember being able to watch storms come in from a distance. Summer thunderstorms were the best. After a hot day playing outside and going swimming, I can remember feeling cozy coming back inside when a thunderstorm would approach during the afternoon heat. There was nothing better. At that point, I had not yet developed the fear of what severe weather was capable of doing. This infatuation with the weather increased as I got older, and in high school, I actually had the thought of meteorology as a career.

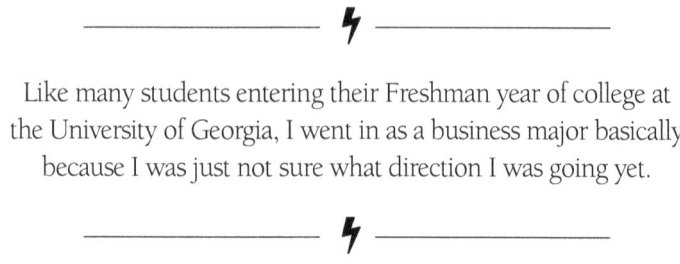

Like many students entering their Freshman year of college at the University of Georgia, I went in as a business major basically because I was just not sure what direction I was going yet.

I knew that the first year was just about the basics anyway, and my two older sisters were trying to convince me to not go into television as they did not think my personality was cut out for it. They were well into their TV careers at this point and thought I was too sensitive to go into such a cutthroat, harsh business. As Hunter S. Thompson said, "The TV business is uglier than most things. It is normally perceived as some kind of cruel and shallow money trench through the heart of the journalism industry—a long plastic hallway where thieves and pimps run free and good men die like dogs, for no good reason." But by surviving and thriving in this industry, I would later prove my family wrong.

Finding My Path

I pledged to a fraternity and, unfortunately, discovered that I loved alcohol. Being sheltered in a small town coupled with a newfound, heavy-duty party life, I was about to flunk out of UGA by my sophomore year. I had not been taught how to study, and college was a rude awakening for me. I was going out almost every night of the week, so I had to make some big decisions. After some soul searching, I realized that I really wanted to pursue meteorology and go into television weather. To do that would require leaving UGA and getting serious about my studies.

In 1990, I moved to Tallahassee, FL. With poor grades and being out of state, Florida State University did not accept me. But I was determined. So I moved down there, not knowing one person and went to Tallahassee Community College to continue coursework that would get me into FSU. One year later, in 1991, I was finally accepted into the meteorology school of FSU. They were in the top five schools in the country for meteorology, so I was extremely excited. I will never forget my advisor and his first words to me. He looked at me and said: "Arch, I can see a twinkle in your eye, and I can tell you like to have fun. Are you ready for this major? It is not going to be easy." I answered, "Now more than ever, sir. "

My Dysfunctional Meteorology School Experience

My drinking did not slow down, but I learned how to study and party. I studied hard and played hard. I learned that if I were to do both, I would need at least five hours in the library studying every night before heading out to the bars. It's amazing how resilient the body is in your twenties. It's very easy to bounce back from a hangover from the night before.

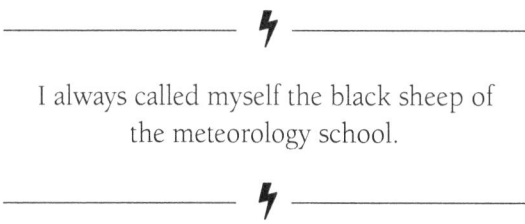

I always called myself the black sheep of
the meteorology school.

Most of the students were ultra-smart nerd types who were going into either research or working in forecasting for the National Weather Service. I can count on one hand how many of us were planning on a TV career path. Little did I know in the beginning that a major in meteorology would require a minor in mathematics and a good deal of physics as prerequisites to advanced meteorology classes. The math was tough, as I had to take every calculus class offered and Engineering Math 1, which included differential equations often referred to as Diffy Q's. I was one class shy of a minor in physics, and all of these classes were required as meteorology is basically a combination of calculus and physics. As hard as it was, it was exciting as I had big dreams, and I really loved studying weather and climate.

In the summer of 1992, before my last year at FSU, I was fortunate enough to land an internship at WAGA in Atlanta, which was a CBS affiliate at the time. There I would learn how to make weather graphics for the chief meteorologist, Ken Cook. I had a blast that summer as my sisters were both now anchors/reporters at two different stations in Atlanta at the time. I lived with Kathleen while I interned and discovered the gay nightlife in the city. I knew this was where I wanted to be one day.

After graduation in the fall of 1993, I packed up my things and moved back home with my mother in Thomaston, Georgia, where I grew up. I was able to make a demo reel during my internship, and I sent copies out to small local stations in Georgia close to home. I had an immediate call back from the ABC affiliate in Macon, Georgia, WGXA, which was only a 45-minute drive east of Thomaston. I interviewed literally the following week home, and only a few days after that, I was offered the job doing their weeknight weather.

I will never forget the first week of work learning a cold hard fact of TV news—you must leave your feelings at the door.

One afternoon preparing for our 6:00 p.m. newscast, I heard my news director yell out in the newsroom, "Yes. We have a murder. " You see, assignment desks listen to police radios for significant news events that are taking place. You could call us professional "ambulance chasers."

In TV news, you get to hear all of the news first. So as shocking as it was to hear the news director say something so horrible, I soon learned that news people looked at tragedies as news stories and had to disconnect the personal aspect of house fires, murders, car wrecks, etc. So the news director looked at the murder as a story, not a tragedy. This was definitely a hard thing to get used to. Another thing that was hard to get used to is not taking things personally, which is hard to do when it is yourself that you are selling.

Moving to Atlanta

I learned so much in the Macon market, and it prepared me for my next job, which was the weekend morning meteorologist for the NBC affiliate in Atlanta. I have my sister, Kimberley, to thank for handing the news director at WXIA my demo reel and putting in a good word for me as a meteorologist. As you find out in most careers, it sure helps to know somebody. But, I don't want to sell myself short. Atlanta was a top ten market, and I knew they were not going to hire someone who couldn't do the job. After a job interview with the news director and the head of the station, they offered me the job. Not only was it exciting at only 26-years-old to be doing weather in a top ten market, but it was also overwhelming as this was the summer of the 1996 Olympics held in Atlanta, and we were the host network. Literally half of the world was in Atlanta watching our news. The energy in the city was incredible, and I will never forget that experience. At the end of my three-year contract, I decided to move on as they did not want to promote me to better shows. I felt that doing only two weekend shows for three more years would keep me from growing in my career.

I would spend the next four and a half years working as a part-time meteorologist at The Weather Channel, CNN, and the number one Atlanta affiliate, WSB. By 2004, I realized I was stagnant and looking back, I know why. My alcoholism had developed during this time, and it was beginning to affect my on-air work. Drinking became a daily event as a way to calm down from work. The next day, the withdrawal would set off panic attacks at work, and it was getting harder and harder to hide it. This was where I was introduced to Alcoholics Anonymous (AA) and began attending daily meetings.

———————— ϟ ————————

After a year of getting my life together, I believe that God opened a door for me, and I walked through it.

———————— ϟ ————————

My Progression from Orlando to Nashville

In the summer of 2004, the ABC affiliate in Orlando, Florida, WFTV, was showing interest in me for the weekend meteorologist position. It was going to be tough, as it was a position of doing both the morning and evening shows on Saturday and Sunday. Basically, no sleep whatsoever for two whole days straight. The good part was that I could get a three-day weekend during the week. Then two of the weekdays, you were to make graphics for the chief meteorologist before starting the grueling shift all over again on Saturday morning. The pay was good, and the station was the number one affiliate in Orlando with the best weather technology of any station around. This was probably the most exciting part of my career. As everyone remembers, and especially Floridians, 2004 was the year that three hurricanes swept through the state—Charley, Frances and Jeanne.

The first hurricane I was ever in was Charley. As it barreled through Central Florida, I recall taking a break from 24/7 coverage and taking a look outside. I have never seen rain blowing completely horizontal through the air. The palm trees resembled ponytails in the wind. Due to the intense wind, I had to use all of my might just to shut the station door. It was quite an experience. The devastation to Central

Florida was astounding. When the storm was over, I will never forget taking off from the airport and seeing a sea of blue tarps on top of most houses from above.

Toward the end of my contract, the weekday morning meteorologist position opened up. I desperately wanted off on the weekends, and I discussed my interest with my news director. After doing heavy research, which stations do profusely, they found another meteorologist who tested better than me for the position. This was devastating to be simply treated as a commodity, so it was very hard not to take it personally. That meant that people did not like me enough. It was at this point that I started thinking of a different career. I was tired of being passed up for higher positions, which I wholeheartedly believed I deserved.

Just as I was about to leave the meteorology business, a chief job opened up for me in the summer of 2007 in Nashville, Tennessee, and I accepted it.

I spent three and a half years as the chief meteorologist in the Nashville market. After fourteen years of working weekends and every holiday, I finally enjoyed a little piece of the pie. My sobriety has allowed me to succeed in a very tough business. I enjoyed the people of Nashville, and I always said Nashville was a medium-sized city with a "big city" feel. I think it is due to the music industry being there. The town was electric. Seeing music stars at the grocery store was a common occurrence, and they acted just like everyone else and were very humble. I will never forget walking through Whole Foods© one day only to look up and see one of my favorite actors, Nicole Kidman, walking hand in hand with her husband, Keith Urban—just like everybody else. No entourage. Just the two of them browsing the aisles. Very cool.

However, as much as I loved my job and the money, I started becoming very lonely. Because Nashville was not a very big city, the gay population was small. Most of the gay people there were usually paired up, so being single and gay there was not so good. I found myself working all week and then sometimes not seeing one person during my weekend. I began to wonder if it was worth it. All my family and lifelong friends were in Atlanta, and I began considering leaving the business and moving home. This decision did not come lightly, and I spent a year contemplating what kind of career change I could make. I was so specialized that I knew I would probably not be able to stay in the TV field or even meteorology, for that matter. Those jobs don't grow on trees.

Moving Home

When I hit forty years old, I decided that I would move home even with no career plan. This was a very bold move on my part because this was in 2010 when the economy was down. Several people thought I was crazy for leaving a high-paying job during the worst economy since the Great Depression.

To this day, I still regret this move occasionally. But then my faith reassures me that God makes no mistakes, and there was some reason this was meant to happen. God has never left me, even though at times, I have left Him. On Thanksgiving of 2010, I moved home to be with my dying mother. I didn't know it at the time, but my meteorology career was dead and buried. The next ten years would prove to be the most challenging and agonizing period of my life, both personally and professionally.

The TV news industry has changed dramatically since I left the business. In the quest for viewership, the news business has leaned toward opinion and sensationalism rather than news telling to gain the shock value to retain viewership. Because of this, many Americans don't trust TV news anymore. And fewer and fewer people are watching it.

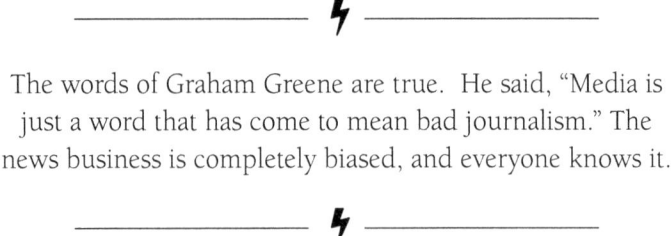

The words of Graham Greene are true. He said, "Media is just a word that has come to mean bad journalism." The news business is completely biased, and everyone knows it.

Also, with advances in technology, people have many different sources of information. Where we once had just three networks to watch at 6:00 p.m. each night, we now have both 24-hour cable coverage on our TVs along with online media at our fingertips.

With so many sources for news and weather, I would assume the big TV salaries are a thing of the past, as we know that bigger ratings drive bigger salaries. I would think, however, for those interested in meteorology, it isn't money that drives that interest but a love for science. As for me, it was a love of weather and being on the pulse of breaking information.

Today, I'm still in the process of establishing a new career, and it has been a rollercoaster ride. As I've expressed throughout this book, it was my most important decision that kept me pressing forward–my spiritual belief and faith in Jesus Christ. His relentless love for me has never changed, so I know I ultimately have nothing to lose as I continue my new career journey.

My Method for Dealing with This Life Challenge:

My career has had many ups and downs, and I would not trade any of them for the world. Why? Because, even during the bad times, I learned something. We never stop learning, and many times it is from our mistakes.

I made a choice to go into television despite being told I was not cut out for it, and I have no regrets. When you are told you can't do something, that can be a reason to pursue your dream even harder. With God, anything is possible.

Also, I am reminded of some great advice from Kathie Lee Gifford. She said, "Find something you love and figure out a way to get paid for it." This truly is the key to a life of contentment. Ask for God's direction to make it happen.

Here's the Truth:

One thing is for sure, weather forecasting is an inexact science and improving technology continues to help us in saving lives and making our quality of life better. There will always be a need for good meteorologists. Despite my imperfect career journey exacerbated by my own actions and those imposed upon me, I am grateful for the time I had in this career.

CHAPTER 4

The Battle for My Mind and Body

"Never underestimate a recovering addict. We fight for our lives
every day in ways most people will never understand."

– Unknown

I was probably 5-years-old when I had my first drink. Don't laugh...
it's true. You see, my parents were having a cocktail party one
night, and after finishing their pre-dinner drinks, they retired to the
dining room to eat. Of course, I don't remember this story since I
was so young, but this is how it was told to me. I must have noticed
the still half-filled glasses sitting out probably looking like different
fruity colored juices to a 5-year-old. I proceeded to go about the room
finishing off the glasses of alcohol—so generously left by the guests.
It must not have taken much because our family doctor, who was
over for dinner, found me out cold on the sofa. He he checked my
vitals to find that I was just passed out drunk. The story is actually
quite funny, but I always found it ironic that I would become a true
alcoholic later in life.

A Late Bloomer That Caught Up

I was a "late bloomer" in high school. All of my friends tried their first beer in eighth grade. We had a "spend the night" party at my house, where my buddies snuck in a few six-packs. We waited until my mother and sisters were asleep, and then they took no time in cracking them open. However, as the youngest child, I was always the do-gooder. Wanting to make my mother happy by being a good child, I was not adventurous at all. It was lucky for me that night that I did not try alcohol, as Kimberley found us and threatened to tell Mom if we did not pour it all out. You want to talk about some petrified young boys? With extreme panic, we all took the alcohol and poured it out in the woods behind our house. I would never even think about drinking until three years later.

It was in my junior year of high school that I came out of my shell. I began to take more chances and got up the nerve to have my first drink as a teenager. My mother started getting sick when I was 10-years-old with severe rheumatoid arthritis, and she required a lot of care even when my sisters and I were growing up. Both my sisters were six and nine years older than me, respectively, so I took care of Mom a lot once they went off to college.

During one of my mother's hospital stays, I had a small party at the house with alcohol. Thankfully, I had some quality friends in high school, so they were very respectful and never damaged my home. It was the perfect opportunity for me to have my first drinking party, and I did. In fact, I had quite a few of them and so many that eventually, I threw them all up later that night. Looking back, I should have known I was an alcoholic. I absolutely loved the extreme inebriation from the very first drink. The feeling for me was euphoric, and because of that sensation, I would continue drinking with my friends through my senior year.

Even though I was coming out of my shell in high school and college, I was still on the shy side. When I got to the University of Georgia, I found that drinking really eased my nerves and allowed me to be social without fear, especially since I was also hiding my sexuality. So, this fact, coupled with these euphoric feelings, contributed to some hard-core drinking in college. As part of a fraternity, there were parties almost every night at the fraternity house or local bars. Sunday nights, though, we took off from drinking. Not surprisingly, my first two years at UGA proved to be unsuccessful—academically speaking. My partying got the best of me. And that, coupled with the fact that my small-town public school had not prepared me well for college studying, I came awfully close to flunking out my sophomore year. So I had to make some decisions.

More Pressure after Changing My Major

I was not happy as a business major, but I did have a secret interest in meteorology, specifically TV meteorology. My two sisters had already begun their careers as news anchors and reporters and had their start in Columbus, Georgia. My interest grew in the weather aspect of news being more scientifically-minded.

After some soul searching, I realized that I had to manage my drinking if I wanted to complete my education. Unfortunately, UGA did not offer meteorology, so I started researching meteorology schools and found that Florida State University was in the top five meteorology schools in the country. Plus, it was fairly close to home. So, I picked up my life, left UGA and headed south to Tallahassee. Unfortunately, my grades were poor, and I could not get into FSU right away, so I took classes at Tallahassee Community College to get the credits that I needed until I could make the transfer into FSU. I found an advisor in the meteorology department by the name of Dr. Henry Fuelberg. I will never forget him. He was my mentor, and I had incredible respect for him in the field of meteorology. I will also never forget what he said to me in my interview for the meteorology school at FSU. He looked me in the eye and said, "Arch, you look like a guy who likes to have fun. Are you sure you want to do meteorology?"

You see, meteorology is a complex major that requires a great deal of knowledge in the areas of mathematics and physics. It's not an easy major. Even back then, my alcoholism was recognizable to people that didn't even know me, including Dr. Fuelberg. Ironically, when I graduated three years later, he was one of the proudest of me for what I had accomplished. I learned to control my alcoholism so that I could earn my Bachelor of Science in Meteorology. I worked hard and played hard. I learned that I would have to spend five hours in the library every evening before I could go out to the bars to drink. As I look back now, I am astounded I was able to get this degree. It is truly amazing how resilient the body is at that age. It was very easy for me to bounce back from hangovers to head to class each day. But, the day came when I had to make another decision involving my drinking and my career. Writer and clinical psychologist, Frank Tallis, sums it up well, "At first, addiction is maintained by pleasure, but the intensity of the pleasure gradually diminishes, and the addiction is then maintained by the avoidance of pain."

Life Becomes Difficult to Manage

As I grew into my twenties, my career and alcoholism took off. I cared about two things: weather and drinking—nothing else. A decade of this destructive behavior would eventually put me at a crossroads.

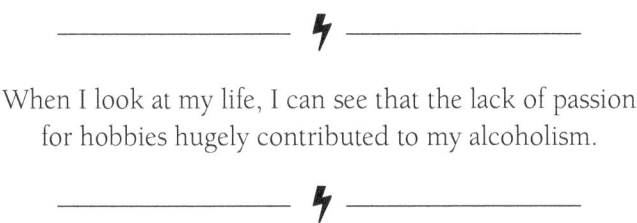

When I look at my life, I can see that the lack of passion for hobbies hugely contributed to my alcoholism.

I began to have severe panic attacks, which actually started in college and grew more severe as my career progressed. In the beginning, I thought it was heart problems, as my heart would race every time an attack started. If you have never experienced a severe panic attack, they are dreadful. It feels like you are going to die, and you can't stop it. This, in turn, causes the heart to race even faster and has a snowball effect. Many times, shaking and sweating occur at the same time.

According to American Addiction Centers, one study reported that 25 percent of people seeking treatment for panic disorder had a history of alcohol dependence. Alcohol has an effect on many chemicals in the brain, including GABA, serotonin, and dopamine and when these chemicals are altered, it can throw off how the body reacts in everyday situations. Alcohol can induce panic because of its effects on GABA, a chemical that normally has a relaxing effect. Mild amounts of alcohol can stimulate GABA and cause feelings of relaxation, but heavy drinking can deplete GABA, causing increased tension and feelings of panic.[3] At age 26, I had extensive heart tests, and the doctor concluded that my heart was in great shape. He brought out one of his medical books, opened it up to Panic Disorder, and asked me to read a paragraph from it. He said, "Is this what you are feeling?" I affirmed, and he diagnosed me with severe panic disorder, and I was put on an antidepressant. This helped but not on days after drinking heavily, which happened about four days a week. Later after I went into recovery, I would find out that what I was experiencing was withdrawal from alcohol.

My Career Takes a Plunge

At age 28, the drinking started affecting my on-air work. I had left the NBC affiliate in Atlanta, where I was doing the weather for the weekend morning shows. It was a great gig for a young person who had only been in the Macon, Georgia market for three years prior. But as my three-year contract ended in Atlanta, it was time to move on to a better position. In television news, it often requires a lot of relocating to move up the ladder in the field. I interviewed at The Weather Channel, which is based in Atlanta, and landed a part-time, on-air position. It was very exciting to be on a national network for the first time, but it was also quite a challenge as one must know a lot of the geography and local nuances of the whole country.

I learned so much there during my short two-year stint, but this was the period when alcohol started to actually affect my career. On my very first day of work, I called in sick. I was too hungover and was having severe anxiety. I would not be able to go on-air. The shame I

---

3   americanaddictioncenters.org/alcoholism-treatment/anxiety

felt that day was tremendous. At this point in my drinking career, I was also dabbling in cocaine, which increased the anxiety attacks to an astronomical level. I always say that cocaine is the best drug for the alcoholic, as it wakes you up so you can drink more. The day I called in sick to work, I was having such bad anxiety that my good friend, who was a doctor, had to prescribe me Xanax to lower my heart rate. He was worried I was going to have a heart attack, and he said we needed to get the heart rate down.

I was at the lowest and darkest point of my life. The drugs and alcohol were getting the best of me, and if I was going to keep my career, I had to at least tone it down, and I did just enough to function. A little wake-up call happened when the man I was dating at the time— a very jealous person—got tired of me going out to the bars and convinced my two sisters to do an "intervention." A favorite watering hole during this time was Blake's in Atlanta, a very popular gay bar known for its earlier crowd. I loved day drinking, and it always had a busy Sunday afternoon crowd. A perfect day for me was heading to a gay restaurant in Midtown Atlanta for brunch and cocktails and then heading over to Blake's for some heavier drinking until I passed out.

One particular Sunday evening, I was there having my usual beers when I turned around, and my two sisters were standing there and telling me they wanted to take me home. As drunk as I was, my heart sank. I could not speak. I was embarrassed for two reasons. First, I had never seen them in a gay bar before, even though at this point, they knew I was gay. Second, I was embarrassed for them to see me this drunk. I always hid this aspect of my life from my family. I went home with them with my tail between my legs, and they sat me down and told me I needed to go to AA. At this point in my life, I was not ready to accept that I was an alcoholic, but I went to a meeting anyway, and you can imagine how it turned out. I went for about a week before I was back at it—drinking and out at the bars on my off days.

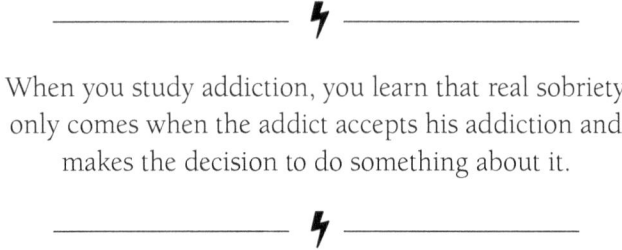

When you study addiction, you learn that real sobriety only comes when the addict accepts his addiction and makes the decision to do something about it.

While interventions can help, usually, the addict must hit "rock bottom" to be open to getting help. Getting sober for someone else never works, at least not for long.

I never drank on the job, but my on-air performance was being affected by the severe hangovers and withdrawal. After two years at The Weather Channel, I was still part-time and decided since I was not getting a full-time gig, I would have to move on. CNN was hiring part-time meteorologists to fill the gaps when needed. I considered it a way in the door that could possibly lead to a full-time position. This was an exciting time because I was at my second national network. But work was starting to suffer, as my body was not handling the severe hangovers from drinking the nights or days before work as I often worked overnights.

I will never forget the day I got a phone call down to the weather office at CNN. The head of the network told me that I better shape up and that I looked dead on air. No one in the industry knew the extent of my drinking... or maybe they did. The alcoholic is always the last to know how bad off he or she is. An opportunity opened up for me at Headline News, which was in the same building and a network owned by CNN. I was filling in on their morning show with Robin Meade after their morning meteorologist left. CNN was doing their research and working on deciding on who was to fill the weekday morning weather position. I wanted the job so badly. After six months of filling in, they gave the job to another male out of North Carolina. I was devastated. This part of my life was so hazy that I can't even remember if I left CNN or if they just stopped using me as a fill-in.

During my six years of part-time work at The Weather Channel and CNN, I was also filling in at the local ABC station, WSB, when the meteorologists were on vacation. Juggling all of these jobs was like working full-time but without the benefits. So for a year, I was working only at the local affiliate in Atlanta when needed and suffering horribly from hangovers at work and severe panic attacks. It was a weekday, and I was filling in for the weekday morning meteorologist. I had completed the morning show, took my break and began to prepare for the noon newscast to finish out my shift. A severe panic attack came on, and I could not get out of it. It was one of the worst I had ever had. My heart was racing, and I felt like it was going to explode. I started hyperventilating and shaking tremendously. It wouldn't stop, so I had to tell them I would not be able to go on air, and the meteorologist on vacation had to be called in to complete the shift. I had to have the anchor of the show get in her car and follow me home to make sure I got there safely. To this day, I still don't know if they knew what was going on with me. I am sure they did but just did not say it.

This was my third and final wake-up call. I had had enough. My life was stagnant. I was not progressing in my career, and I was miserable.

I would have to make a choice—drinking or losing my career. Actress Jamie Lee Curtis said, "Recovery is an acceptance that your life is in shambles, and you have to change it." I chose to get sober, which possibly saved my life. In 2003, I proceeded to an AA meeting which, of course, I had already been introduced to thanks to my sisters several years earlier. Interestingly, after a year of sobriety, my career really started to take off. Amazing how that happens, isn't it? The decade of my thirties proved to be the most successful years as a meteorologist.

Getting My Life Back

At the end of my first year of sobriety and daily AA meetings, I got a call from WFTV, the Cox Communications in Orlando, Florida. They knew I was at WSB in Atlanta as a fill-in as Cox Communications also owns WSB. The Orlando station had an opening for a weekend meteorologist. Even though the pay was equal to what I was making part-time in Atlanta, it was a full-time position and at the number one station in that market which was a good career move. The next three years proved to be probably the best of my career in TV.

It was during my first year that we had three major hurricanes move through Central Florida. It was a meteorologist's dream. I learned a lot, continued to grow in my career, and my work took all of my time. I traded my alcohol addiction for a work addiction. As a weekend weatherman, I was not only doing my job but also filling in for the weekday meteorologists when they were on vacation. I had found a good AA group, and I was pretty regular my first year in Orlando. But as my job took more and more of my time, I drifted away from the program. By my second year there, I was not even going to meetings. As a "workaholic" now, I did not have time to think about drinking. It honestly never crossed my mind. That incredible work experience later landed me a chief meteorologist position in Nashville, Tennessee, at WZTV, where I spent the next three and a half years forecasting the weather. It had now been almost eight years of abstaining from alcohol, and I had no desire to pick it back up.

At 40 years old, I was making more than I ever had in television, but I was not happy. As a gay single man in Nashville, it was not the best place to live because the gay population there was small. The people of Nashville were wonderful, but the loneliness was getting the best of me. After a lot of thinking, I decided to leave TV news and move back home to Atlanta. I wasn't sure what I was going to do. I just knew that money wasn't enough. I longed for companionship—both in a committed relationship and with close friends I could have when I was not working.

Persisting Bad Choices and Challenges

I had never been in a long-term relationship and was intensely lonely. And after a year of being home in Atlanta, I met someone. He was masculine, which was very attractive to me. You would not have known he was gay unless you asked him. Also, another incredible quality is that he had a great head on his shoulders. So many men I had met in the gay world were very unstable. Many have drug and alcohol problems, while others can't have monogamous relationships.

Leon was easy-going and a downright good person. We hit it off, and after a year, we found ourselves on a trip to Ft. Lauderdale with friends. I will never forget the day. It was a sunny day on the beach, and Leon and I were lying on the sand, and I noticed a Fat Tuesday's on the boardwalk.

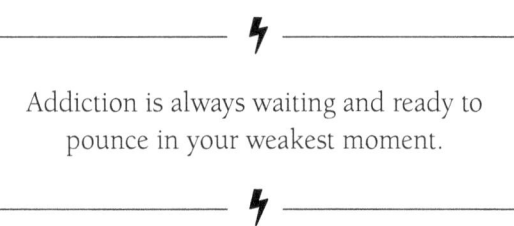

Addiction is always waiting and ready to
pounce in your weakest moment.

According to the National Institute on Alcohol Abuse and Alcoholism, "There is evidence that approximately 90 percent of alcoholics are likely to experience at least one relapse over the 4-year period following treatment."[4] I had a thought, *I am now about 10 years older and have, for the first time in my life, a partner who I think will be with me for a lifetime. I think I can actually handle my alcohol now.* The years of frequent panic attacks and withdrawals were a distant past, and I had forgotten how bad it was. Leon did not really know the extent of my past alcoholism yet, and he was not a big drinker. He could have one or two, and that was all he ever needed.

I convinced him I would like to try again, so we proceeded to the bar and ordered a drink. The buzz was wonderful, sitting in the sun with that frozen fruity drink. I had forgotten how good it felt. Leon was a bit unsure what to do but went along with it. We may have had two drinks that day, and that was it. It took only six months, and I was right back where I was before I got sober and went into AA.

---

4   pubs.niaaa.nih.gov/publications/aa06.htm

The drinking got more and more intense, and eventually, I ended up in a detox hospital for the first time just eight months after picking up a drink again. During this time, my mother's life was slowly coming to an end. Her rheumatoid arthritis had made her bedridden her last 13 years of life, and Kimberley and I were caring for her along with someone we had hired on a full-time basis. Mom could not feed herself, go to the bathroom, or basically do anything for herself. She had become completely helpless, and it was taking its toll on everyone. Looking back, I have to think that this contributed to my alcoholism even though I loved my mother deeply. She was my life, and to watch her suffer for so many years was excruciating for me. My heart could not take it, and I am sure alcohol eased that pain.

My forties were the darkest days of my life, and I can say without a doubt that I have gone through the worst part of my life. As Mom was slowly dying, I would go in and out of detox hospitals and rehab facilities while Kimberley and I continued to care for her. I have never endured such pain as I did during that time, and alcohol certainly wasn't helping matters. I could not seem to stay sober and was feeling utterly hopeless. One of my most depressing times was one Easter Sunday when I was locked up in rehab and looking out the window early that morning alone with strangers and not being with family celebrating what was the most important day of the year for me next to Christmas Day.

Leon and my family were at the end of their ropes, and I was about to be on the street. It does not get much lower than that.

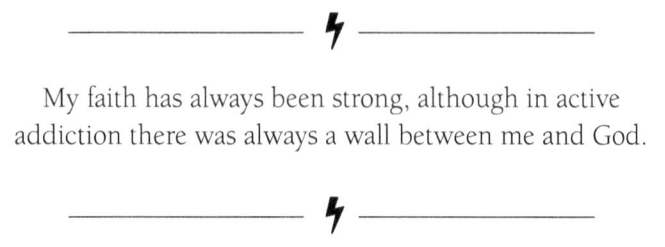

My faith has always been strong, although in active addiction there was always a wall between me and God.

I know that must hurt God so much. He wants to walk the journey with us every step of the way. God did not leave me, and He had a purpose for me. The time between relapses got shorter and shorter until, eventually, my body had had enough. Singer Demi Lovato obviously reached the same point when she said, "One of the hardest things was learning that I was worth recovery." I was at my lowest point, and I did not have another drink in me. The bad finally completely outweighed the good, and I would find myself truly "sober" for the first time. You see, you can be a "dry" drunk, but that does not bring contentment. To be content, one must be a "sober" drunk. American dancer, actress, and choreographer Anne Fletcher has it right when she says, "Nobody stays recovered unless the life they have created is more rewarding and satisfying than the one they left behind."

It took me 50 years to learn this fact, but God still had a purpose for me. As a man of faith, I believe wholeheartedly that God uses our pain for good in the end. Otherwise, what is the point? If you don't believe that, then life makes no sense. God kept me alive through seven detox hospitals and two emergency rooms for a reason. That reason is to help others with addiction and also to make a life and career for myself that glorifies God. I'm reminded of this quote that says, "Recovery is not for people who need it. It's for people who want it."

In my research, I came across the credentials of the CAC, which stands for "Certified Addiction Counselor." It is a two-year curriculum offering a wealth of addiction and treatment knowledge. One of the biggest takeaways from the program is that you learn that addiction is a disease of the brain that cannot be cured. But it can be managed just like diabetes, heart disease, etc.

We have PET scans that can show us a lot about what is happening in the addicted brain, which provides proof that addiction is a brain disease. Yes, a person has a choice in the beginning, but after a certain amount of time, an addict no longer has the choice. The drug of choice rewires the brain, and the addict "needs" the drug to survive daily living. This describes why two people can drink excessively in college, one becomes a full-fledged alcoholic after college, while the other person resumes normal life activities.

When you study addiction, you find that there are solutions, and nobody has to die of addiction if they get to the point that they truly want help. Another sad aspect of addiction, however, is that only about 25 percent of those seeking help stay sober for life. Most at the very least relapse, while many die.

But if we can save just one life we encounter, is that not worth it? I believe it is.

My Method for Dealing with This Life Challenge:

My faith tells me that I can use the pain in my life to make something good, that the suffering shall not be in vain. God kept me alive for a reason. As I have walked through my post-TV meteorology career, I have been searching for my purpose. I am still on that search, but I do know that a part of it will be to help other addicts. It may not be as a career, or maybe it will be. That is not the point. I can share my story with anyone who is addicted that God brings into my life. It is about giving others hope.

There is still a stigma regarding addiction. Unfortunately, many today still believe it is a choice, and it indeed is in the beginning. But there comes a point where it is not a choice anymore, and the brain "needs" the drug to survive. We still can't predict who will become an addict after their first use of the drug. Genetics can play a big part, so it is desperately important for parents to educate their children at an early age if the family has a history of addiction. While we have no control over what our children eventually do, we can at least rest in the assurance that they were taught about the potential of addiction that hides in their genes to enable them to make the best decisions possible.

Coping with her own illness, Mom did not have the ability to really educate me on alcoholism in our family. I have alcoholism on both sides of my family, and it wreaked havoc on us growing up. Alcohol made my grandfather verbally abusive, and alcohol eventually killed him. I don't remember much about Dad's drinking as I was very young before my parents got divorced. But I remember Dad getting very quiet on evenings of drinking, retreating to his bedroom, and shutting the door. I think as children, we all think we are invincible, so we take that first drink blindly. Alcoholism in my family history was the last thing on my mind when I began drinking more heavily in high school. Literally everyone was trying it. Why wouldn't I?

This led me to excruciating pain throughout my life, but again, I don't see it as being in vain. I was listening to a very prominent doctor who specializes in addiction medicine. He talked about the dismal numbers of those who truly recover from addiction, but he said after years of funerals of clients he lost, if he saved just one, it was well worth it. I agree.

1. If you're a parent, talk to your children about the dangers of addiction.

2. If you're in the midst of an addiction battle, don't do it alone. Ask for help.

3. Relapse is often part of recovery. Get back on the horse and try again.

One major caution for addicts is to be very aware of trading your addiction for another one. Addiction replacement is very common in addicts as one searches for another way to feel the same high one achieved from the previous drug of choice.

Signs of addiction replacement are:

- Constantly thinking about your new activity or vice.
- Losing sleep to participate in the new activity.

- Trouble at work, school, or at home.
- Relationship issues with a spouse or loved ones.
- Neglecting self-care and personal hygiene.
- Experiencing stress or anxiety if unable to complete the new activity.[5]

Here's the Truth:

We know so much more now than we ever did about addiction, and it is a brain disease. The good news is that while one is never cured, addiction can be managed like many other diseases.

---

5   addictioncenter.com/community/addiction-replacement

CHAPTER 5

The Unlikely Yet
Unapologetic Politician

*"If you believe in something, you need to have the
courage to fight for those ideas – not run away from
them or try and silence them."*

– Charlie Kirk

I never really cared about politics growing up. Even into my twenties, as my career took off, weather was my only passion. I came from a moderately conservative, Christian, southern family. I can't remember much discussion around the dinner table on the topic of politics and religion, but we were brought up to respect everyone and to put God first.

Church was a must every Sunday morning, and a coat and tie were required to show respect for our Creator. Despite my family's dysfunction and shortcomings, I never heard a racist word or curse word from my parents' mouths. Racism was foreign to me in the small Central Georgia town of Thomaston, with a population of only 9,000

God-fearing people. White and black people would socialize together at school, and nobody seemed to see or judge people by the color of their skin from what I witnessed.

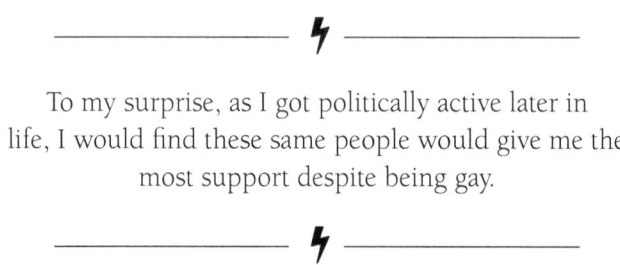

To my surprise, as I got politically active later in life, I would find these same people would give me the most support despite being gay.

My Political Interest Grows

As I made my way to Nashville as a chief meteorologist for the local Fox station there, I suddenly grew a deep interest in politics. Barack Obama started his service in 2009 as the President of the United States. He had charisma, and much of America was thrilled to see a Black President for the first time in history. Despite being technically biracial, the social justice warriors considered this to be enough.

I began to notice some radical ideas and moves on his part as he took the presidency. Spiritually, I noticed things like Jesus Christ being left out of speeches and Islam used as a replacement. It was very apparent that he wasn't basing his political decisions on his faith in Jesus Christ. His rhetoric was anti-police and divisive. This was very disturbing for me, and I truly believe that despite his polished prose, he instigated the incredible divisiveness in our country today. He started a race war.

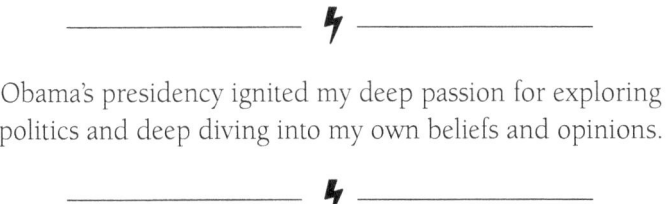

Obama's presidency ignited my deep passion for exploring politics and deep diving into my own beliefs and opinions.

As I started doing my research, I watched more national cable news and began reading more than I had ever done in my life. Glenn Beck's message and perspective captured my attention. He was new to the cable news scene with a gig on Headline News. I loved his freethinking. He was definitely conservative, but he was also not afraid to voice his opinions even if they deviated from the Republican agenda. I respected that, and here are just a few of my favorite quotes from him:

"Sometimes the hardest part of the journey is
believing you're worthy of the trip."

"We should reject big government and look inside ourselves
for all the things that built this country into what it was."

"Political Correctness doesn't change us, it shuts us up."

"Every time the government grows we
lose more of who we are."

"It's not just spending, it's not just taxes, it's not just
corruption, it is progressivism, and it is in both parties. It is
in the Republicans and the Democrats."

"Progressivism is the cancer in America and it is eating
our Constitution, and it was designed to eat the Constitution,
to progress past the Constitution."

"I beg you, look for the words 'social justice' or 'economic
justice' on your church website. If you find it, run as fast as you
can. Social justice and economic justice, they are code words."

"Good for you, you have a heart, you can be a liberal. Now, couple
your heart with your brain, and you can be a conservative."

He was able to help one really think for oneself and establish one's
own thoughts and decide which side of the aisle you were on. I read
his first book, *The Real America: Messages from the Heart and Heart-
land* and I was hooked on politics.

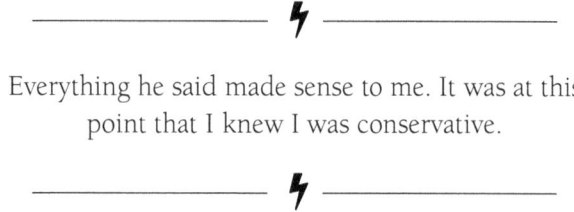

Everything he said made sense to me. It was at this
point that I knew I was conservative.

Beck then led me to Sean Hannity and then to my ultimate hero, Rush
Limbaugh. In turn, these on-air conservatives would then lead me to
authors like Ann Coulter, Peter Schweizer and Nabeel Qureshi, where
I would continue to drink up their thoughts and information daily
for the coming years.

My Gay Marriage Outing

Fast forward to 2015. The Supreme Court makes gay marriage legal in all fifty states in *Obergefell v. Hodges*. At this point, I had been following politics vigorously for five years, so I was pretty knowledgeable on what was going on and how both Republicans and Democrats operated.

I had been watching Facebook friends openly post their strong political opinions while remaining quiet about mine for years, and I had finally had enough. I had always tried to keep my opinions private, as I never wanted to stir up any argument with friends. Drama has never been my thing, but I could no longer hold back.

For the first time, I posted my opinion on gay marriage on Facebook.

I expressed my agreement that the LGBTQ community should have the same legal rights as straight people who made a monogamous commitment to another human being, but that I disagreed with the way it was done. It was an intentionally sugar-coated, non threatening post.

What I didn't say publicly is that I believe in the Bible's interpretation of marriage, which is between a man and a woman. Genesis 2:24 states: "That is why a man leaves his father and mother and is united to his wife, and they become one flesh."

Here are some additional scriptures on marriage:

"If a man marries a woman who becomes displeasing to him because he finds something indecent about her, and he writes her a certificate of divorce, gives it to her and sends her from his house, 2 and if after she leaves his house she becomes the wife of another man, 3 and her second husband dislikes her and writes her a certificate of divorce, gives it to her and sends her from his house, or if he dies, 4 then her first husband, who divorced her, is not allowed to marry her again after she has been defiled. That would be detestable in the eyes of the Lord. Do not bring sin upon the land the Lord your God is giving you as an inheritance." (Deuteronomy 24:1-4)

"It has been said, 'Anyone who divorces his wife must give her a certificate of divorce.' 32 But I tell you that anyone who divorces his wife, except for sexual immorality, makes her the victim of adultery, and anyone who marries a divorced woman commits adultery." (Matthew 5:31-32)

"Some Pharisees came to him to test him. They asked, 'Is it lawful for a man to divorce his wife for any and every reason?' 4 'Haven't you read,' he replied, 'that at the beginning the Creator 'made them male and female,' 5 and said, 'For this reason a man will leave his father and mother and be united to his wife, and the two will become one flesh'? 6 So they are no longer two, but one flesh. Therefore what God has joined together, let no one separate.' 7 'Why then,' they asked, 'did Moses command that a man give his wife a certificate of divorce and send her away?' 8 Jesus replied, 'Moses permitted you to divorce your wives because your hearts were hard. But it was not this way from the beginning.'" (Matthew 19:3-8)

With respect to government, I believe that, like all laws, gay marriage should have been passed through a bill in Congress. I stated in my post that the Supreme Court is supposed to *interpret* law, not *create* it. Also, it is my opinion that with respect to legal rights, both straight and gay people should have "civil unions" when it comes to domestic partnerships. This would ensure that the definition of marriage as stated by God in the Bible would remain protected. It would also hopefully satisfy the gay community concerned with human rights. This one post changed my life forever.

As a meteorologist in Atlanta in the late nineties, I was well known in the gay community because I was also quite a partygoer at the gay bars and also easily recognized from being on one of the local news stations. For the most part, I knew everybody who was gay in Atlanta. Needless to say, I was connected to most of them on Facebook years later. I was shocked by what happened next.

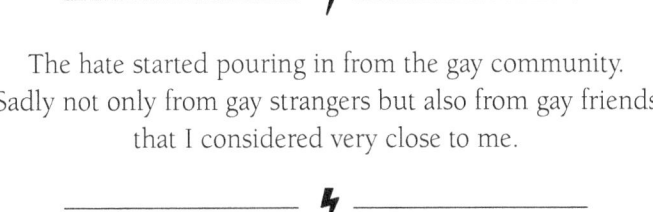

The hate started pouring in from the gay community.
Sadly not only from gay strangers but also from gay friends
that I considered very close to me.

The first emotion was shock, then hurt, then anger. You would have thought that I had killed their dog or something. I was called everything in the book—everything from self-loathing to an alcoholic, to a washed-up, has-been weatherman, and much more. I would continue to get hate messages privately and on the open forums of Facebook. I find it ironic that the one group that preaches tolerance the most is the least tolerant group of them all. Over the following months, I lost most of my gay friends. This fueled rage in me, and I always say the leftist gay community created a monster because every bit of hate coming from them only drove me to become more politically active.

Making the Right Decision

While I became very isolated and sad, there was also a great sense of relief and peace in finally expressing myself. I had always chosen to keep my mouth shut to avoid confrontation, but that was no more. Here is some more good news. The isolation was short-lived, as I began to connect with other gay conservatives around the country on Facebook, and I realized that, while I was a minority within a minority, I was certainly not alone. I found gay conservative chat groups and was even fortunate enough to start meeting other like-minded gay conservatives in person.

As I began seeing the increasingly leftist radical behavior in the Democrat Party, I posted more and more, feeling a need for online activism to counter some of this radicalism in my own little world of followers.

My Political Beliefs

Today we are witnessing an ever-increasing divisiveness in our country and a seeming decline in those who believe in our founding principles of the Constitution. Unfortunately, the Democrat Party is nothing like it was 20 or even 10 years ago. Make no mistake that the party has left God and put government and social justice in His place. What is most disturbing about the party today is totalitarianism. The Left no longer allows debate, and they are canceling any challenging thought. This is very dangerous; you cannot have a free society without free speech and debate. Social media is the new "town square," and Big Tech is censoring any conservative opinion.

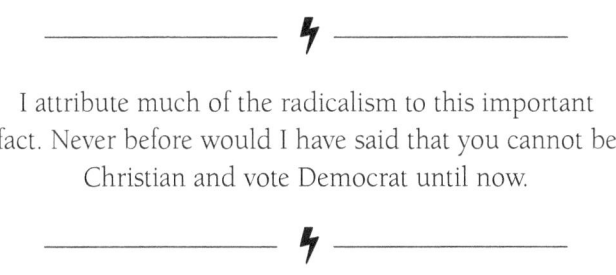

I attribute much of the radicalism to this important fact. Never before would I have said that you cannot be Christian and vote Democrat until now.

Don't believe me? Just look at two important topics the Democrat Party stands for: abortion on demand up until birth and completely ignoring immigration laws. If you read the Bible in Romans 13, you will see that God says we must obey government laws, and I think abortion up until birth speaks for itself.

So here we are with a Democrat Party that has moved radically left and censored conservatives beyond reproach. Big Tech is stifling free speech for conservatives. With social media being the new town square, conservatives are not allowed a voice as part of their First Amendment rights. In my opinion, the solution has become painfully obvious, and that is that it is time to break them up like we did with the Bell system back in 1982. This is one monopoly that could become an enormous cost for our great country—the cost of freedom.

For a free society to exist, we must let everyone have a voice. The totalitarianism of the Left and not allowing dissenting opinions must stop if we are to have any semblance of what this country was founded on.

My Method for Dealing with This Life Challenge:

Why is conservatism better for our country and our world? The main reason, in my opinion, is because so-called "liberals" have left God completely. The Democrat Party 20 years ago encompassed many Christians who were open to debate with Republicans. Not today. Government and the Climate Agenda are their gods. The Democrat Party is one of totalitarianism where debate is not allowed, nor is a deviation from groupthink. Those who think differently are canceled and deemed irrelevant. Conservatives are individual thinkers who welcome debate. We must have an open society where everyone has a voice, or we will not stand as a country, and America will fall. Thankfully, Democrats like Bill Maher have spoken about this cancel culture, and he has warned his fellow Democrats about the danger of totalitarianism. But more Democrat leaders need to speak out on this to save our free and open society that is becoming anything but that today.

Here's the Truth:

We need to come back to our creator, God, as a country. We became the greatest country in the world because we were founded on Judeo-Christian values. We must return to those values.

CHAPTER 6

Caring for My Beloved

"Caregiving often calls us to lean into love we
didn't know possible. To care for those who once
cared for us is one of the highest honors."

– Tia Walker

Mom wasn't always bedridden. She enjoyed physical freedom as a child. But, although she physically felt fine, it was not a happy childhood. Mom watched her mother try to commit suicide right in front of her. Her mother did not succeed, but it left an emotional scar, that of course, would never heal. It's amazing that my mother's mental health turned out to be so good as an adult. She had a mind of steel contrasted with her very fragile body.

To add insult to injury, my mother's father was busy building a very successful career, eventually becoming President of Gordon Foods. The drawback to his success meant a lot less time spent with her, but one saving grace was her extended family. Paw Paw's three sisters would fill a void that would give her some sense of love and support. Also, my mother enjoyed a happy college life pledging to the sorority Pi Beta Phi at the University of Alabama before eventually meeting the love of her life, my dad, Arch Jr.

Stresses That Added to My Mom's Disease

I have very few memories of my mother walking. In the early 1960s, she was in her mid-twenties when she was diagnosed with rheumatoid arthritis, an auto-immune disease. I was born a few years later. Mom started feeling pain in her hands first. She continued to have three children despite her disease, and she would miraculously go into remission while she was pregnant with me.

My mother was 30 years old when she had me in 1970, her last child, and it was after my birth when her disease really pushed full steam ahead. At 40 years old, her body began to succumb to the crippling effects of the disease, which put her in a wheelchair. The heartbreaking reality is after her diagnosis in the 1970s, there was not a lot of advancement in the treatment for severe rheumatoid arthritis. Her only options were doctors prescribing aspirin and gold shots she would periodically receive, which helped very little. In 1988, a new drug treatment surfaced called Methotrexate. We were hopeful, but at this point, she was so advanced that the disease had already damaged her joints. She was severely crippled. This may be a surprising statistic. Seventy-one out of every 100,000 people are diagnosed with RA every year, and about 1.5 million Americans are living with rheumatoid arthritis. Interestingly, women are about two to three times more likely to get RA than men. Thankfully, today those diagnosed with this disease have advanced medical treatments to prevent the severe crippling of the joints that is a direct result of RA.

To make matters more devastating, I was 10 years old when my parents got divorced. My oldest sister, Kimberley, was heading off to college while my other sister, Kathleen, was in high school. Kathleen was driving us home from school one day, and she said, "Archie, I have something to tell you, and it's not good. Mom and Dad are getting divorced." I was stunned. The timing could not have been worse as he left during the time when Mom's cornea was burning out, which is often a side effect of rheumatoid arthritis. She would have to undergo a corneal transplant. Alone. He had obviously fallen out of love with her, and I suppose most of it was because of her illness.

I'm also convinced that Dad's drinking further contributed to their separation. Apart from my parent's relationship, as a child, all I can remember when he would drink was that I feared him. He got very quiet when drinking, and I can remember him getting a very stern look on his face that scared me. As a pilot for Delta, Dad would have a schedule of three days on and three days off. During those three days at home, he would fix his first drink at around 5:00 p.m. By dinner, we would sit at the dinner table in silence, and then I remember him heading off to their bedroom and shutting the door for the rest of the evening. It was not a happy household.

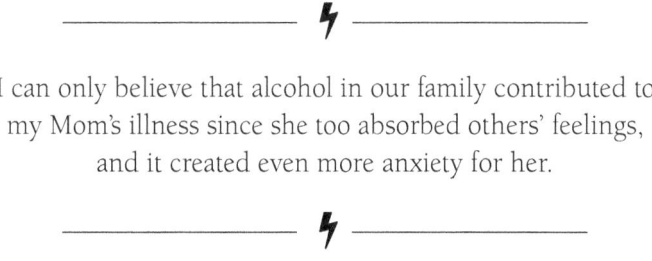

I can only believe that alcohol in our family contributed to
my Mom's illness since she too absorbed others' feelings,
and it created even more anxiety for her.

Every member of our family was challenged in ways none of us expected. We were all operating in stress behaviors, and for me, it was a way of life that would continue for many years to come, which undeniably contributed to my alcoholism as a coping mechanism.

My mother's father, whom we called Paw Paw, was an alcoholic. He lived close to us on the farm he bought after retirement. Retiring early, I am convinced, led to his extreme alcoholism as he had a lot of time on his hands. He was a very successful businessman who made his way to the top, coming from a poor beginning. I believe his strong Type A personality was the reason for his success but also his downfall in the end. He would be doomed by the denial of his disease of addiction. Eventually, his liver shut down from his alcoholism which caused his death at 74. His drinking was from morning till night with a bottle of Cutty Sark in the glove box of his Lincoln Town Car and his bathroom cabinet.

I still vividly remember the smell of tobacco and whiskey on his breath. Because of his high tolerance to alcohol, he never appeared drunk. But, his verbal abuse toward all of us was through the roof. I was an immensely sensitive child, and he took advantage of that. He would often make fun of me by telling my friends that I was scared to play football. They would laugh, and I would feel very embarrassed. Once I remember him making me get out of the car and then act like he was driving off. I ran toward the car as he pretended he was leaving me. One night I recall, we were over at his house for dinner, and he put me outside the kitchen door and turned out the carport lights to scare me. All of this was funny to him, but it did irreparable damage. My mom would often say, "I wish you had known him before his drinking. He was such a great man." Unfortunately, at his advanced stage of alcoholism, I never knew that man.

The mental abuse from my father and my grandfather did a number on all of us. But, I truly believe my mother's disease of rheumatoid arthritis would not have been so extreme without this extra stress. So, it was a double-edged sword when Dad left, and Paw Paw died. Yes, Mom's heart would be broken, but she would no longer have the daily stress of mental abuse. None of us would.

My Mother's Continued Decline

During my high school years, it was just Mom and me. Both my sisters were away at college, and Mom's disease continued to worsen. We spent most of our life with Mom at Piedmont Hospital in Atlanta, either at doctor appointments or in surgeries. First, Mom had her toe joints replaced. It actually seemed to work, but it was only feet. Many other problems surfaced.

One problem in particular that really had an impact was when she got both knees replaced. They have come a long way with this type of surgery today, but it was a new frontier for doctors in the early 1980s. Needless to say, the surgeries did not work. Because of her illness, she had to go a certain number of weeks without any knees at all. She would be bandaged up lying in bed for weeks before the prosthetics could be put in. I remember sleeping with Mom at night so we could make a train to the bathroom. She would wake me and hold on to my waist as we walked to the bathroom, where I would wait until she finished, and then we would train back to the bed. Eventually, the knee replacements would prove to be ineffective, and she was back in the wheelchair. As her disease progressed, the problems got more serious and life-threatening. Do you know what it is like to wake up every day as a child wondering if your mother was going to die that day?

Mom loved to shop. We would make time for the grocery store and the mall, but she began to become very nervous appearing in public. Children would always stare, and I could see her expressions when it happened. It devastated her. Her crippled joints were very obvious and probably quite shocking to people who had not experienced such a severe case of rheumatoid arthritis—especially children. Mom's little hands were curled under and that is what probably was most evident to people. Initially, I would feel embarrassed at being stared at when we were out with her in the wheelchair, but eventually, the staring was something we just ignored. It was life. You adapt.

Mozell – My Second Mother

We had a housekeeper named Mozell, and she has been with us since I was in diapers. She called herself my "Black Mamma." She was part of my life, and she truly was a second mother to me. As Mom got sicker and sicker, Mozell took on more of a caregiver role as well as house cleaning. I don't know what I would have done without her after my sisters left for college.

I have fond memories of Mozell, and through the heartbreak of Mom's illness, we had some fun times together. One, in particular, was her fear of thunderstorms. We basically lived in the middle of a pasture, so our home was in the wide open with very few trees around us. I loved watching thunderstorms roll in from a distance, but Mozell did not. She was terrified of them. In fact, I loved to tease her when she would say there was "coming up a cloud." She literally would not leave the house after work until the storms completely passed. We had many laughs and enjoyed being silly together.

Another very fond moment with Mozell was when the WSB helicopter landed in our front yard on the farm. Kimberley was an anchor at WSB in Atlanta during the 80s and 90s and was very good friends with an investigative reporter, Mark Winne. He had been at a story not far from our farm and had the pilot land the helicopter in our front yard to stop by and say hello. Mozell was in awe. She could not wait to get her picture taken in front of the chopper. And seeing her pure joy could not have pleased me more.

Throughout my four years of high school, Mom would sometimes be away from home for weeks at a time. She would be in the hospital for different surgical procedures, and Mozell would make my dinners for me to have at night. Once I was driving, I could manage by myself. I could make my own breakfast and lunch, but as a kid, I needed help with the dinners. Mozell was my family, and I cherish and miss her every day.

Caregiving During My College Years

I think one of the hardest times for me was going off to college. I got accepted to the University of Georgia and was very excited but also fearful. I was such a homebody and had anxiety about leaving home, although the newfound freedom was also exhilarating. That fall, when it was time to check into my dorm, Mom just happened to be in the hospital for surgery.

My best friend in high school was Murray Deen. His mother, Betty, was also like a mother to me. During my early years, she did many physical things for me that my mother could not do, and I am forever grateful to her. I loved Betty—or as I used to call her, Bugga—like my own mother. She took me and checked me into my dorm since Mom could not. I will never forget that. I was so nervous because not only was I leaving home for the first time, but I was also very worried about my Mom. In fact, I lived my life constantly worried about her. Looking back, this is probably why I had such a hard time leaving home. I was so scared, but Bugga gave me comfort that day.

During my college years, Mom did not need 24-hour care yet. Mozell continued to be her nurse. And eventually, we had to hire someone else to do the housework so Mozell could stick to just helping Mom with everyday things that most of us take for granted. I was always just a car ride away from home, which was in Thomaston, Georgia, as I transferred from the University of Georgia to Florida State to pursue a major in meteorology. I remember driving home a lot of weekends to see Mom and help her with things and just be with her. We were closer than most mothers and sons, and I believe it was for two reasons: her illness and my being gay. I often hear that most gay sons are closest to their mothers. At least for me, that was true.

After college, I was fortunate to get my first two jobs in TV close to home. So Mom, being home-bound for the most part, could watch me and "critique" my work on air every night. Starting in Macon, Georgia, which was market 120 at the time, I made the jump to Atlanta three years later, which was market 10. Between my two sisters and me, we could take turns being there for Mom, whether it be hospital stays or doctor visits.

Debbie — A Gift from God

In 2004, I got a fantastic job opportunity in Orlando, Florida, and for the first time, I was ready to really leave home. I had been sober for about a year at this point, and we were lucky to have found Debbie. She lived in Thomaston, Georgia and was looking for part-time work and had no problem spending nights at the house to take care of Mom.

To this day, I believe Debbie was a gift from God. It was so incredibly hard to find someone we could really trust to take care of our mother since she could literally do nothing for herself. Before Debbie, we thought we had found a good candidate, who eventually stole from us, taking some of Mom's jewelry and some of the grandchildren's toys. Since my sisters lived an hour away from Mom in Atlanta, they could not keep a 24-hour watch on what was going on. It was a very delicate situation. So we cherished Debbie, and she really became one of the family.

Debbie tended to lighten the mood often. She could be incredibly fun to be around. We spent many a night around the kitchen table at dinner just cracking jokes and telling funny stories. What made Debbie so different was that she actually loved living with us. How many people do you know who can actually pick up their life and not only live with another family but literally mold into their life like they were just another family member? Debbie did just that and made life so much easier. One more light moment during Mom's decline was another instance around the kitchen table. Because of her disease, Mom could not use the computer, so she knew little about websites and how to navigate them. As we were discussing posting to social media one night, Mother advised us to post some pictures to "MyFace." For a split second, we all looked at each other with a blank expression, and then began laughing hysterically—realizing what she meant. Not being able to use the computer, Mom confused the social media sites "Myspace" and "Facebook." It was a good laugh at her expense, but she was a good sport about it.

I would have had a hard time leaving Kimberley if Debbie had not been with us. It took a tremendous load off of us. I still managed to fly home a lot from Orlando to see Mom. With Debbie around, it was kind of nice to be able to just enjoy Mom without having to be constantly concerned with what needed to be done next. We could just be with her. But Debbie still needed breaks and vacations. During this time, Kimberley picked up the slack when Debbie was on vacation. Another unhealthy dynamic of this situation was that Kimberley had a codependence on Mom. When I look back, my perception was that Kimberley liked it better if Debbie was gone so she could have more control of the relationship with Mother. Because she had never married, Kimberley relied on Mom emotionally. Mom was the sounding board for her victimhood because Mom was a captive audience, and Mom relied on her physically.

Caring Long-Distance from Nashville

After three years in Orlando, my career then took me to Nashville, where I landed a chief meteorologist job and spent the next three and a half years. It was a three-and-a-half-hour drive through the mountains, and was very nice coming home on some weekends to Atlanta. Again, thanks to Debbie, I was able to pursue my career without too much worry about Mom. I was very thankful because, for a while, Mom was physically able to make the car ride up to Nashville, and Kimberley and Debbie would bring her every once in a while, and they would stay the weekend. At the time, I was very appreciative of Kimberley for bringing Mom, but as complicated as family relationships can many times be, I would later come to believe that she was not doing it for me but only for Mom.

I was becoming very lonely in Nashville, as I was single, and weekends alone in the house got very monotonous. At 40 years old, I made a life-changing decision. I decided to leave television and move back home to Atlanta to be near family and a few old friends who still lived there. As much money as I was making, it was just not worth it.

All the money in the world makes no difference if you
have no one to share it with. I do not believe God created us
to be alone. Humans are meant for companionship,
so I chose that as my first priority.

After a year of contemplating the move, I did it during the crazy time in 2010 when the economy was really low. People lost their homes and jobs, and here I was, leaving a well-paying job to move home because I was "lonely."

Loneliness was not the only reason, however. Mom was getting really bad at this point. When Debbie took days off, Kimberley had to fill in, and I knew it was starting to affect her life even though she spent all of her time with Mom anyway. It was now taking a lot of physical effort. Debbie and I were the only ones who could pick Mom up out of the bed and put her into the wheelchair to take her to the doctor or to wash her hair. So, if Debbie was gone, Mom did not get out of the bed—sometimes for over a week.

Mom's Health Spiral

After moving home in 2010, Mom started really spiraling down. Her last three years of life were in complete agony for her physically and for us emotionally. I had picked up alcohol again and went in and out of detox hospitals in between taking care of Mom. Even though I am responsible for my actions, I know that the stress of my mother's illness and Kimberley's control and manipulation issues aided my alcoholism. And I'm certain that my lack of availability was hard on Kimberley as well.

Mom literally couldn't even scratch her own nose if she had to. Because she could not do anything for herself anymore, she was extremely scared to be left alone and with good reason. Dialing the phone was impossible. Things got really bad during Mom's last year of life. Debbie got married, and we were left without any help. Kimberley unleashed on Debbie, letting her know how horrible it was that she was leaving us. Kimberley seemed to love chaos and was also good at pitting people against each other. She tried to make Kathleen and me mad at Debbie for living her life and getting married. So, Kimberley and I took over, and it got very stressful.

When one of us wanted to get out just to go to the store, the other had to be there. Kimberley would not allow Mom to hire anyone else because she did not want the inheritance money to spent on anything that we could do.. Kathleen and I knew that was the case. In fact, Kathleen even said to Mom, "Hire some help. Paw Paw left you the money to do that." She was right. That was what the money was for. Mom would not do it and chose to rely totally on Kimberley and me. In fact, for most of our life, Mom would rely mostly on Kimberley and me as we did not have spouses. With no children of our own, our time could be devoted totally to Mom's care. It was obvious to me that Kimberley had a mental hold on Mother because of Mom's physical dependence on her. They were completely dependent on one another.

Being completely bedridden, Mom was a captive audience for Kimberley and her troubles. With Kimberley's constant complaining about how bad her life was, I believe it took a huge toll on Mom's illness. This made a stressful situation all the more stressful for me. God got me through all of this. And I know, without a doubt, that I would not have made it out alive without Him.

The Worst Day of My Life

Mom passed away in her sleep one morning as I was at a job interview. I will never forget the worst day of my life and the phone call from Kimberley, crying hysterically, saying Mom was dead. The day I dreaded most was here. Dad was at the house with Penny, my stepmom, and I was very thankful because it comforted me.

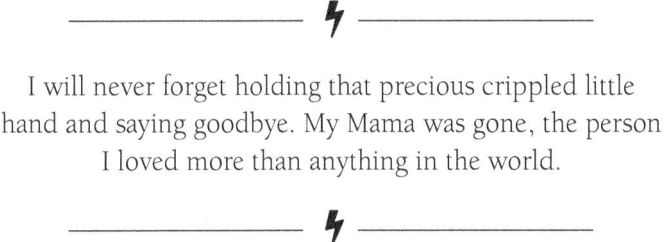

I will never forget holding that precious crippled little hand and saying goodbye. My Mama was gone, the person I loved more than anything in the world.

What transpired a week later was a complete shock, something I had never dreamed would happen and had only seen in movies. Kimberley and I were at the breakfast table eating lunch in Mom's house a few days after her death, and I mentioned that I would like to take Mom's car, of course, since I didn't have one at the time. Her face went pale, and she was just silent. I said, "What's wrong?" She wouldn't speak, and I said, "Kimberley, you are scaring me. What's wrong?" She answered, "We should just wait until the reading of the will." I remember thinking how odd that statement was. I knew there was a will reading, but I thought it was a no-brainer about the car.

My heart sank because I knew how important money was to Kimberley, and something was just not right. Later, my mind took me back to an actual funny moment between us many years back when I was living with her after just getting a job in Atlanta. Back then, we paid bills with checks, as there was no online payment system yet. One month we were paying bills, and when the cable bill was divided, she gave one of us one more cent to pay; she gave that penny to me. We both laughed, but the deeper issue was not so funny. Even back then, this was a perfect example of how money-conscious she was. Questions started arising in my mind. Could Kimberley have tampered with Paw Paw's will? Could she have been that money hungry?

The Pain Continues

The day of the will reading was a sad day for me. It solidified that my Mom was gone and reopened the fresh wound of her passing. Kathleen, Kimberley, and I rode to the lawyer's office together. I did not know the attorney. The whole thing just felt really weird, and I didn't know why.

Here's a little background. Paw Paw basically left his money to Mom in a trust, and his will stated that the money was meant to take care of her. When she died, the trust was to be split equally between the three grandchildren. What Kathleen and I did not know is that a year before Mom died, Kimberley had convinced Mom in her deep sickness that she was destitute, would never get married and would "need" the money more than her siblings. Kimberley was also good at playing the victim and always claiming she did more than us helping Mother. And there was a reason for that, as I would soon discover.

The odd thing is that Kimberley is an attractive, healthy, and intelligent woman who made a great living her whole life as a television anchor. Still, she was able to have Paw Paw's trust dissolved and the will changed to have 80 percent go to her with 10 percent to Kathleen and 10 percent to me. I had seen fictional movies where this kind of thing happened but not in a million years would I have ever dreamed that my own sister would do this to her siblings.

I never even thought about Mom's money during her life. And it was so sad to me that Kimberley would not only worship money but also be so calculating and manipulative before Mom died to make sure she got it all. Also, I never thought about who did more for Mom. Mom was my world and even when I would get tired of doing things for her, I loved her more than anything and calculating how many more hours I spent taking care of her was foreign to me. I never even once had a thought in my head that the money should not be divided evenly like our grandfather had wished. It was his money and Kathleen was his grandchild too. Businessman and automaker executive, Lee Iacocca, was quoted as saying, "No matter what you've done for yourself or for humanity, if you can't look back on having given love and attention to your own family, what have you really accomplished?"

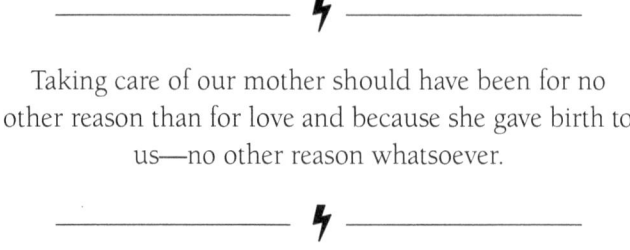

Taking care of our mother should have been for no other reason than for love and because she gave birth to us—no other reason whatsoever.

Mediation Steps

I will be forever grateful to my brother-in-law Joe and sister Kathleen for facilitating us into mediation to try to get Kimberley to see the error of her ways. Kathleen knew what Kimberley did was wrong, and I am forever grateful to have a sister who I know loves me without a doubt.

Kimberley didn't budge in mediation–not even a little. And finally, we just gave up, not wanting the lawyers to eat up all of the money in long-term disputes. Eight years have gone by, and not a word from Kimberley. During this time, she got married and actually sent an invitation to the wedding to Kathleen and her children but not to me. The only reason I can think of why she did not send one to me is that she knows she hurt me the worst. Kathleen has a husband to take care of her, and they do well financially. I had lost everything after I left TV, and Kimberley knew it. Oh, yes, and what happened to Mom's car? Kimberley sold it and used the money to pay for new countertops in her house to get it ready to sell. Why did she sell her house? Because she also got Mom's new house, too. So, not only did she take 80 percent of Paw Paw's trust, but she took Mom's house and car.

Forgiveness and Reconciliation

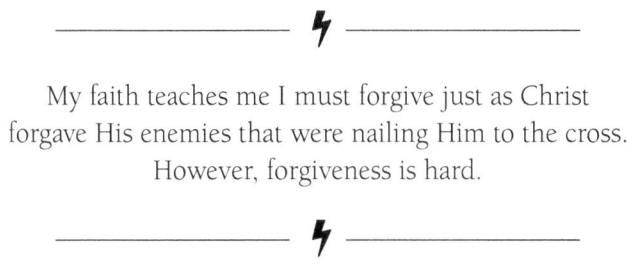

My faith teaches me I must forgive just as Christ
forgave His enemies that were nailing Him to the cross.
However, forgiveness is hard.

They say that family hurts you the most, and that statement is so true to me. I think it is because your family knows you best and knows how to go for the jugular vein and hit you where it hurts the most.

Mom's illness brought out the worst qualities in each of us. I realize that now, and I am not without sin. The biggest shock to me from everything in my past was Kimberley dissolving the trust and taking most of the money away from her two siblings. Above anything else in my life, this decision has been the hardest thing to forgive. What hurt the most was the fact that I had lost everything and "needed" the money. Every financial stab, such as taking the car and buying new countertops for her home, was the icing on the cake. It was unbelievable.

But as Christ forgave those nailing Him to the cross, so must I forgive Kimberley and everyone else who commits sins against me. I know this in my mind and heart, but it is the hardest thing to do. Well-known speaker Iyanla Vanzant says, "Family is supposed to be our safe haven. Very often, it's the place where we find our deepest heartache."

My sister Kathleen and I talk about this and ask ourselves, what does forgiveness look like? That is the million-dollar question. What does forgiving Kimberley look like? Does it mean I call her up and strike up a sibling relationship like nothing ever happened? Do I let her back into my life? Do I not hold her accountable for not doing the right thing? These are all important questions I ponder every day.

I know forgiveness is ultimately for my benefit, not the other person's. I know I cannot thrive in life, resenting others who have harmed me. But does that mean that I allow Kimberley back into my life? Possibly so, but with boundaries. Certainly, we cannot have a relationship as it was, with her constant manipulation and need for control. I know that if she did the right thing, gave the money back, and admitted what she did was wrong, I could welcome her with open arms. But that might not happen. So what do I do? My faith is telling me I must forgive and move on and better my life to the best of my ability—and that is what I will do no matter what happens.

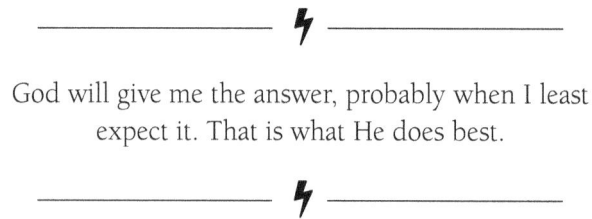

God will give me the answer, probably when I least expect it. That is what He does best.

It took me a long time to forgive my Dad. I thank God daily that our relationship is mended as I get older and realize how true it is that life is short. When he left, it was at the worst time possible.

Dad and I have never had a real conversation about their divorce. I think my biggest resentment is having been put in the middle.

Every holiday was miserable because I had to fight with Dad every year about why I was going to be with my sick mother on Christmas

Eve and Day. It was wrong to put me in the middle. Dad had gotten remarried. My mother was sick in bed with no one but her children during the holidays. I was not going to leave her on Christmas.

Mom was not without fault either. She made it quite hard as well during these times. She would have preferred I never saw Dad at all, and I think that was unfair. As much as our situation angered me, I still loved my dad and wanted to see him. She hated that and certainly let me know it. This tug of war went on all through my teens and through college. It wasn't until my first job in TV that I had some "holiday relief."

I will never forget my first job in Macon and the first Christmas Eve and Day I had to work. You see, the news doesn't stop just because it's Christmas. Someone has to read the news and do the weather. Sitting in a Waffle House eating breakfast on Christmas morning because it was the only thing open was very tough that first Christmas without my family. But, I can remember a certain relief in the fact that I did not have to worry about who would be angry at me for not being home for the holidays. I had an excuse. I had to work.

Dad is a completely different man today. He stopped drinking years ago, and now I know a different Dad—the real Dad. He has never brought up the past, but I can see that today he is sorry for how things went down. He never missed an alimony check for years after their divorce. Subtle things this Navy pilot does and says tells me he cares, and that is enough for me. Forgiveness is for me, not for those I feel have wronged me. I believe I have finally gotten there, and what a wonderful place to be. Praise God.

What I've Learned

I never dreamed in a million years that my own mother would allow Kimberley to do what she did. The only thing I can conclude is that Mom depended so much on Kimberley both physically and emotionally that she just gave in and let Kimberley dissolve Paw Paw's will because she was just too tired to fight back. She was exhausted by Kimberley's whining and constant claiming of victim status. This is what I choose to believe. Otherwise, the only other solution is that my mother did not love me. I cherished my Mom. As a gay man, I never had my own family, and my mother was my life. And as tired as I would get from being her nursemaid all of my life, I still would have rather been a nursemaid than not have had her in my life at all.

I regret to this day ever getting angry at her for her constant demands for help. I think she knew that my lashing out sometimes was just from exhaustion from caretaking. At least, I hope she knew. The hard part about forgiving my mother is that she is dead now, and this will always be an unresolved issue since I cannot just ask her. I have to believe that she loved me, and I have to forgive.

My Method for Dealing with This Life Challenge:

My faith tells me that we can always derive something good from bad experiences in life. Otherwise, what is the purpose of anything? I am certainly not the only person that has spent a long time caring for a loved one. But spending a lifetime doing it, I learned a lot of things.

First, I am certainly an imperfect person. I often got tired of driving Mom to doctors, practically living in hospitals, putting the wheelchair in and out of the car, and picking Mom up and placing her in cars and chairs. I would get angry and lash out at her when she couldn't help it. I am deeply remorseful about that. But God knows I was doing my best.

Secondly, just as God forgives His repentant children, we must forgive one another. I would have rather had my mother and care for her all of those years than not have had her at all. That being said, her illness brought out the worst in all of us. My siblings and I saw the worst attributes that each of us represent. The stress of caregiving took its toll on us all and our relationships. Kathleen and I believed Mom should have used Paw Paw's money for more physical help, especially toward the end. But Kimberley did not want the trust money depleted, and now I know what her true intentions were. Forgiveness is a must, however, if we are to live healthy, spiritually fit lives. I know that. And this road to forgiveness is incredibly hard for me. But, I also know that God wants me to thrive and succeed and that will only happen with true forgiveness.

Daily morning prayer has been the key to life for me. I have to level with God because He knows me more than I even know myself. One cannot hide things from our Creator, so honest prayer must occur daily. Only then can one be truly free and live the life that God intends for us.

Thirdly, my sisters and I have always had a hard time asking for help from others outside the family. I have learned that we should not be afraid to ask for help from people that we love and that we know love us. We should have done that more. Little things like this could have lessened the stress just a little.

Fourthly, I have also learned that stepping back and just taking a breath sometimes can do a world of good. All of us can get overwhelmed in life even with normal daily activities, but with caregiving, it can certainly happen a lot more often. Breathe. I loved this anonymous quote that says, "Like airplane passengers, let's not forget to put on our own oxygen masks first. We are no good to our loved ones if we collapse under the strain." When times are tough, taking a pause and coming back to the task at hand is a must for our sanity and wellbeing.

Finally, I have a tremendous gift for absorbing others' emotions. This allows me to empathize with people and their joy or suffering, which is a double-edged sword. This was greatly detrimental to me through the years of watching my mother suffer. I always felt what my mother felt, and it was as if I was going through the same thing. It was Mom's nature to be full of anxiety, so it transferred to me.

I fully believe that this contributed to my alcoholism through the years. The alcohol was a means of escape. To those with addiction tendencies, when caring for a loved one, you must take time to look at yourself and frequently check in with yourself. The stress of caregiving can take its toll on anyone, so an addict must be extra careful and really nurture their sobriety. I found out the hard way.

Here's the Truth:

Long-term caregiving can bring out the worst in a family. The key to overcoming resentments is to truly forgive those whom you feel have wronged you. Only then can you be free and able to prosper.

CHAPTER 7

A Life-Changing Pattern Is Born

"Tell me what you eat, and I will tell you what you are."

– G.K. Chesterton

Fitness and nutrition became important to me for two life-changing reasons. The first reason is watching the most important person in my life, my mother, slowly die and wither away from a debilitating disease. The second reason is the destruction caused by active alcoholism, which shortens and substantially reduces the quality of life.

Because of these profound experiences, I've come to appreciate and cherish the gift of good health. In fact, it has become a life-saver for me.

My Mother's Health Battle

My mother started having pain in her joints in her early twenties and was diagnosed with rheumatoid arthritis at this early stage of life. It's a dreadful autoimmune disease for anyone who has experienced or witnessed it. Mom's joints started crippling in her thirties, and by her early forties, she was already in a wheelchair. Back in the 70s and 80s, when she started getting so sick, the drugs to combat this disease had not been discovered yet. So, all the doctors could really do was help her manage the pain.

Mom hated to take medication, and the most she ever took for years was aspirin. We were always amazed at her high pain threshold. She never took anything stronger, and it is perhaps why she lived as long as she did. If she had succumbed to opioids, she may have died much sooner than 76 years old. By the time my mother was in her wheelchair, I was barely in my teens. So, I hardly even remember my mom walking. After giving birth to me at 30-years-old, she began deteriorating quickly. Miraculously though, she actually went into remission while pregnant with me.

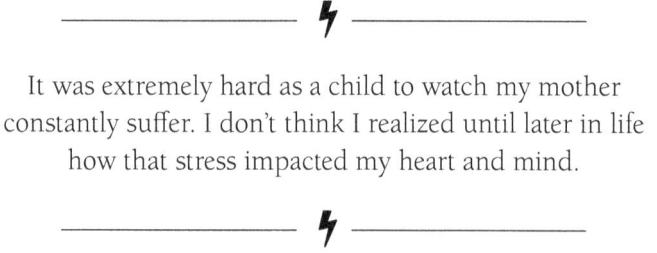

It was extremely hard as a child to watch my mother constantly suffer. I don't think I realized until later in life how that stress impacted my heart and mind.

We spent many days in Piedmont Hospital in Atlanta for doctor's appointments and operation after operation. When a family member is struck with a debilitating disease, you come to really appreciate good health and don't take it for granted. I never have.

In addition to Mom's physical battle was the mental stress my grandfather put on my mother, which I am convinced accelerated her disease and made it worse. A person's state of mind has much to do with physical diseases. Studies have shown that negative influences and thinking not only make a disease worse but can actually create disease in the body. As the Cleveland Clinic reports, "If you don't control high stress levels, chronic inflammation can accompany it and can contribute to the development and progression of many diseases of the immune system such as arthritis, fibromyalgia, lupus, psoriasis, and inflammatory bowel disease." To say Mother had chronic stress would be an understatement.

Conversely, positive thinking and positive influences have been known to slow and even prevent some diseases. In one study by the National Institutes of Health, a community-wide sample of healthy adults from ages 18–50 years old found that lower cumulative stress is associated with better health.[6]

My Battle between Alcoholism and Health

After going in and out of detox hospitals and two emergency rooms for alcoholism over 10 years, I developed a deep appreciation for good health. It doesn't take a rocket scientist to understand the poisonous effects that alcohol has on the body, mind, and spirit. Scientific researcher and author Mike Adams says, "Today more than 95%

6   ncbi.nlm.nih.gov/pmc/articles/PMC4548889

of all chronic disease is caused by food choice, toxic food ingredients, nutritional deficiencies, and lack of physical exercise." And I would add addictions to his list.

On my second visit to detox, my doctor called me in with results from a blood test. He said, "Your liver enzymes are high." My heart sank. I asked, "What does this mean? What do I do about it?" His answer was simply, "Quit drinking." So obvious but so hard to do as an alcoholic.

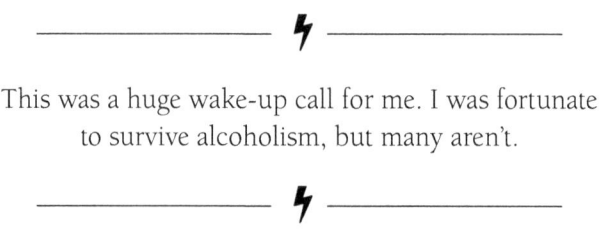

This was a huge wake-up call for me. I was fortunate to survive alcoholism, but many aren't.

Once you get to the point of cirrhosis, there is little hope except for a transplant—and the transplant waiting list is a long one. Additionally, for a liver transplant, a person must stop all alcohol intake for at least six months to be eligible. My grandfather died of cirrhosis of the liver, an all too common ending for many alcoholics and a tragic way to go. His addiction was so great that he was willing to die for it. After my last drink, I vowed never to have an end like my grandfather. Watching him suffer that type of death impacted me greatly, and I will never forget it.

Alcohol drains your mind, body, and spirit until nothing is left but a shell of a body only existing to get the next fix. But, there is good news. Even though addiction is a disease of the brain, and you are never cured, it can be treated by abstinence and learning how to cope with life with complete reliance on God.

A Focus on Healthy Living

In sobriety and after the death of my mother, healthy living has become a passionate hobby of mine. While I don't agree with everything that naturopathy and homeopathy offer, there is much to gain from both. I'm not opposed to using modern medicine to get well, but I also strongly believe in exhausting every natural remedy first and going to medicine only as a last resort.

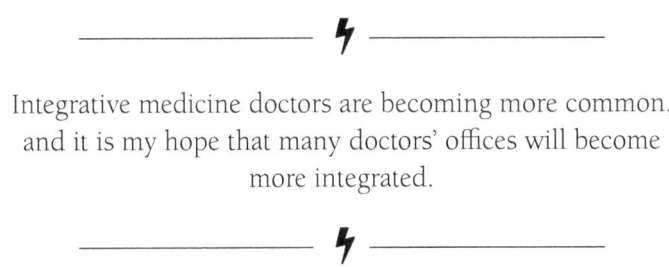

Integrative medicine doctors are becoming more common, and it is my hope that many doctors' offices will become more integrated.

There is a healthy balance, I believe, between conventional medicine and holistic medicine that can give people not only longer lives but longer "healthier" lives. Just as I vowed that I would never die like my grandfather, an agonizing alcoholic death, I also don't want to die a long agonizing death like my mother. She suffered for years, and granted, there was nothing modern medicine could do for her at the time. We know so much more today, and we can do so much naturally to impede the development of many diseases or at least make them less severe. But, the mind is a huge part of it.

When you're drinking, you lose key vitamins and minerals that give you energy and a healthy body. For the body to heal, not only should the drinking stop, but you also need B and C vitamins.

My days in sobriety include healthy eating, supplementation, exercise, and grounding. It's amazing what you can do in your twenties that does not work in your fifties. One of those things is eating fast food. I haven't touched it in several years. That change alone allowed me to lose 30 pounds. As we all know, the body's metabolism slows as we get older, and thus the pounds start adding up. Along with eating better, I have learned that we need supplementation in addition to healthy eating habits. Bodybuilder, personal trainer, and author Karen Sessions says, "Most people don't have a problem going on a diet. The problem is being consistent on their diet."

Supplementing with Supplements

In my opinion, the soil used continuously in farming has depleted the nutrients in our vegetables, even if we're eating them regularly. As we get older, we need to supplement with B vitamins as well as vitamin C and D. Our bodies are unique, so a blood test for vitamin deficiencies can be a great help in determining what you actually need.

I've also personally learned during the COVID pandemic that it can't hurt to take vitamin C, D, and Zinc daily for our immune system to help fight off viruses as serious as flu and COVID-19—especially for older adults and those with compromised immune systems. While the jury is still out on just how much this supplementation can help in preventing COVID, a meta-analysis published in the journal Clinical Nutrition, ESPEN, showed that vitamin D supplementation was associated with a 45% lower rate of getting intubated and, on average, a 1.26-day shorter hospital stay.[7]

---

7   clinicalnutritionespen.com/article/S2405-4577(22)00002-X/fulltext

For addicts in sobriety, my perspective is that exercise is also very important in helping to reset one's body and keeping it healthy. Exercise is great for brain disease recovery. For someone who has suffered greatly from anxiety and depression from alcohol abuse, I can attest to the benefit of exercise. The reason it is so important for addicts in recovery is that it helps the brain stimulate its own "feel good" chemicals, which helps in preventing relapse. Exercise also helps with long-term recovery as replacement therapy. We addicts are constantly searching for the great feeling that the drug of choice brought us. Exercise is a way to feel good naturally rather than artificially from drugs.

Finally, I have discovered a technique called grounding, also called "earthing," which is simply walking barefoot outside. The jury is still out on its overall benefits, but some studies have shown that this is a great way to get antioxidants from the Earth. Grounding or earthing is therapeutic because it focuses on realigning your electrical energy by contact with the Earth. There's not a great amount of research on grounding, but some smaller studies have shown benefits for inflammation, pain, mood, and more. At the very least, it is getting you outside 30 minutes a day with fresh air and natural sunlight.

Through these health and wellness experiences in my life, I've learned the importance of balance and making good nutritional choices.

Sleeping and Fasting

I would have to say that the two things that I have noticed the most positive results would be getting the right sleep and fasting before bed. BK Shivani,[8] author, and engineer describes the best time for sleeping to get the most restorative sleep as between 10:00 p.m. and 2:00 a.m. This has to do with the body's circadian rhythm. The National Institutes of Health describe circadian rhythms as "physical, mental, and behavioral changes that follow a 24-hour cycle. These natural processes respond primarily to light and dark and affect most living things, including animals, plants, and microbes."[9] Basically, it boils down to sleeping when it is dark if you can. I go to bed at 9 pm every night. I wake up at sunrise feeling completely rejuvenated. Just by doing this alone, my energy level increased tremendously.

Secondly, fasting five hours prior to bed has done more for my weight loss than any diet I have ever tried, and I have tried many. The key is eating your biggest meals early in the day. Dinner should be light and done 5 hours before bedtime. The Mayo Clinic says, "After you eat, it takes about six to eight hours for food to pass through your stomach and small intestine."[10] Also, Verywell Health discusses: "Eating a meal too close to bedtime may actually harm your sleep, especially if it's a large amount of food."[11] This is because the digestion process can affect hormones and the circadian rhythm. And, of course, we all know carbs are your enemy when trying to lose weight. It goes without say-

---

8   BK Shivani - youtube.com/watch?v=IwAZn4O6sb4

9   National Institutes of Health - nigms.nih.gov/education/fact-sheets/Pages/circadian-rhythms.aspx

10   Mayo Clinic - mayoclinic.org/digestive-system/expert-answers/faq-20058340#:~:text=After%20you%20eat%2C%20it%20takes,move%20through%20the%20entire%20colon

11   Verywell Health - verywellhealth.com/eating-before-bed-3014981

ing that if you go to bed on carbs that you aren't burning off, they are going to be stored as fat.

My Method for Dealing with This Life Challenge:

What's the key to a good life? To have a healthy mind, body, and spirit, I have learned firsthand that the spirit cannot be healthy with an unhealthy mind and body. Nothing taught me this better than being in active addiction. Spiritually, addiction put a wall between God and me. One is unable to have a relationship with Christ when your brain needs nothing but to achieve the next fix. Physically, the body must mend itself in recovery, and once that is achieved, the attention can be focused on a full spiritual relationship with Jesus Christ.

With respect to other diseases, such as my mother's rheumatoid arthritis, genetic predisposition played the biggest role. Just as important, studies have shown that negative influences and mental abuse can certainly exacerbate an illness as it certainly did with respect to the alcohol use in our family. I fully believe that Mom's illness would not have been as severe if she had had a happy home with full support.

Here's the Truth:

I believe that we aren't guaranteed a life free from illness. However, we can most certainly lessen the severity or even eliminate illness with positive thinking through a healthy mind, regular exercise, and a strong faith in God which gives you the peace that His will be done.

CHAPTER 8

My Method for Overcoming Challenges

"All you need is the plan, the road map, and the courage to press on to your destination."

– Earl Nightingale

So, you've read my story. Now, what do you do with all that I have shared? I believe if you follow and practice the following 13 steps on a daily basis, you can change your life for the better. Mindfulness is huge. When we remain mindful of the things we do to make bad situations worse or keep us in a rut and unable to move forward in life, we can begin the transition to a better way of daily living that will bring a sense of fulfillment and contentment that we never could achieve before. We have peaks and valleys in life, and how we handle both directly impacts us in many ways.

The mind is the key component to the management of life's ups and downs and especially during difficult times and low points.

Without a healthy mind, we cannot work on the body and spirit. It took me half of my life to realize this crucial point. Once you make the mind healthy, you can begin working on the physical and then the spiritual parts of your being. And yes, "all three" are necessary for a life of contentment. How do we get a healthy mind? In review, I told you that nutrition and sleep are crucial to healing a very sick mind or even for renewing a not-so-sick mind that just seems to be in a rut. The benefits can be seen very quickly, and then you can work on a daily ritual that will give you a life you never imagined you could ever have.

The major theme of my book is overcoming life's challenges. Through my personal and professional experiences, there are some consistent steps that form my method—my guide for living.

Here they are:

1. **Prayer** - Start every day with prayer. Ask for wisdom and develop the Fruits of the Spirit[12] to control your emotions.

2. **Positivity** - Always derive something good from bad experiences in life. Use the pain in your life to make something good so that the suffering is not in vain.

3. **Forgiveness** - Forgive those who have wronged you. Only then can you be free and able to prosper.

4. **Truth** - Seek God's truth, and then find your personal voice and have the courage to share it with others in love and respect.

---

12   The Fruits of the Spirit are mentioned in the Bible in the book of Galatians, Chapter 5, Verses 22 and 23.

5. **Trust** - With God's guidance, trust the journey even though you may not know the next step.

6. **Resilience** - When you get knocked down, you get back up. Never hold on to regrets.

7. **Perspective** - Don't compare your life to others. You never know what others are going through or what they will go through in the future. People only post the great points of their life on social media. Don't look at social media as "reality." It is often far from it.

8. **Support** - Surround yourself with those who lift you up and with those you aspire to be like.

9. **Sleep** - Proper sleep is crucial to the healing and restoration of the mind and body. Make the necessary changes to achieve healthy sleep.

10. **Goals** - Set realistic goals for your dreams. A goal is a dream with the steps to get there.

11. **Values** - In a world of "us vs. them," continue to remember what values you stand for.

12. **Faith** - Everything that happens, good or bad, is God's plan. Remembering this can give tremendous peace. What you do with the bad is what matters.

13. **Prayer** - End your day with prayer.

The wonderful thing about this method is that you can make these changes at any point in your life. If you are young, you may be able to avoid much of the pain I went through. If you are older, you can live your best life now. After all, today is all we have, right?

As a recovering alcoholic, I never dreamed I could feel as good as I do today. Many addicts have altered their brain chemistry so much that it seems hard to ever feel happy again. But it can happen. The constant relapses of many addicts are that constant search for a good or even a decent feeling.

I do believe that once you have healed the mind, that search ends, and the chance for relapse is greatly reduced. But this healing of the mind does not just apply to recovering addicts. Many of us have had clinical depression and have felt there was no hope or no way out of the constant feeling of sadness and not being able to figure out why.

This method works, and I am living testimony of it. It will work for you with practice and perseverance, too! Ask for God's guidance and then truly listen for His response. You will receive a life you never imagined possible.

Chronological Timeline

1960 - My mother was diagnosed with Severe Rheumatoid Arthritis and begins having pain in her joints.

1970 - Arch was born. Mom was 32 years old and RA went into remission with pregnancy. My two sisters are 6 and 9 years old.

1976 - Arch tries alcohol as a child not knowing that the drinks were not juice.

1980 - Parents divorce as mother's health continues to decline, specifically her cornea burns out as well as deterioration of her joints.

1986 - Arch has first intentional use of alcohol and likes it very much. Mother's health continues to decline.

1988 - I graduated from high school.

1988 - I had my first same sex sexual experience.

1988 - I attend the University of Georgia in the Fall. Methotrexate is first used for RA but does very little good for Mom, as her disease had already done its damage.

1989 - My alcohol use intensifies in college.

1990 - Upon almost flunking out of UGA, Arch gets his life together and transfers to Tallahassee Community College. My grades were not sufficient to enter into Florida State University (FSU).

1991 - I got accepted into the Meteorology School at FSU.

1992 - I got my Summer internship under Ken Cook, the Chief Meteorologist at WAGA in Atlanta.

1990-1993 - I continued drinking and partying while coming home many weekends to be with my sick mother. Mom's arthritis continues progressing with surgeries being a regular occurrence.

1993 - I graduated from FSU with a Bachelor of Science in Meteorology and a minor in math. Arch returns home to Thomaston to live with his mother while searching for his first job in TV.

1993 - In the Fall, I began my first job in television at WGXA in Macon as a weekday meteorologist.

1994 - On New Year's Eve, I tell my mother that I'm gay.

1996 - I got a job as a weekend morning meteorologist at WXIA in Atlanta during the Olympics.

1999 - I leave WXIA to pursue better job opportunities. I got part-time work at The Weather Channel and WSB TV in Atlanta. My mother is placed on a ventilator for one week and almost dies.

2001 - I leave The Weather Channel for part-time work at CNN and Headline News with continued part-time work at WSB.

2003 - I quit drinking and joined Alcoholics Anonymous (AA).

2004 - I got a full-time job in Orlando doing weekend weather at WFTV.

2004-2007 - My career took off and sobriety settled in. Mom begins to need more care, and we hire Debbie to take over some of the caregiving to help Mozell. Debbie is hired full-time to live with Mom. Mom is completely bed ridden at this point, and Debbie and I are the only ones who can lift Mom out of the bed to the wheelchair and car.

2007 - I got the chief job in Nashville at WZTV, continued a very good sober life, and continued coming home many weekends to be with Mom. She was able to make several trips to Nashville to see me on some weekends.

2010 - I decided to leave TV and move back to Atlanta. Mom's health continued a downward spiral.

2011 - I continued to take care of Mom along with sister Kimberley. I met Leon at the end of the year.

2012 - I began dating Leon and started back on alcohol several months into the relationship. Leon was not aware of my past alcoholism.

2013 - In just six months, my alcoholism continued to progress to the level when I first discontinued use in 2003. Mom's health continued to spiral and move toward death. I had a hospital detox this year at Peachford Hospital and my second and third detoxes at Anchor with a 28-day program.

2014 - Mom died, and Kathleen and Arch found out Kimberley had dissolved the trust and taken 80% of my grandfather's money intended to go equally to the three grandchildren. Kathleen and I do not have a relationship with Kimberley from this point forward.

2014-2020 - Arch proceeded to go in and out of detox hospitals and rehab facilities including two emergency rooms. Leon and I stay together.

2021 - I leave alcohol at the beginning of the year for good and resume sobriety. I also began to work on this book.

2022 - This book is published, and I begin my new career as an author and speaker.

Special Resources

Here are some helpful resources that have helped me, and they address the topics that I've covered in the book:

Career and College Education

eoas.fsu.edu

noaa.gov

weather.gov

ametsoc.org/index.cfm/ams/education-careers/careers/career-guides-tools/meteorology-fields

weather.gov/media/bro/outreach/pdf/
CareerOpportunitiesMeteorology.pdf

Political Activism

logcabin.org

getoutspoken.com

glennbeck.com/glenns-books/an-inconvenient-book

glennbeck.com/glenns-books/arguing-with-idiots

amazon.com/How-Talk-Liberal-You-Must/dp/1400054192

amazon.com/Demonic-How-Liberal-Endangering-America-ebook/
dp/B004IK8Q8Q

harpercollins.com/products/clinton-cash-peter-schweizer?variant=3
2128423002146&utm_source=aps&utm_medium=athrweb&utm_
campaign=aps

amazon.com/Red-Handed-American-Elites-Helping-China/
dp/0063061147

Addiction

aa.org
nida.nih.gov
samhsa.gov

Caregiving

comfortkeepers.com
caregiver.org
usa.gov/disability-caregiver

Christian Faith and Sexual Orientation

amazon.com/Still-Time-Care-Churchs-Homosexuality-ebook/dp/
B08P3ZSRMT

youtube.com/watch?v=tgCpRNfBzys

purposedriven.com/the-book

biblestudytools.com/topical-verses/bible-verses-about-homosexuality archkennedy.com/2019/03/01/my-thoughts-on-the-united-methodist-church-same-sex-marriage-ban

youtube.com/watch?v=oIMVNrdq9F8

Health and Nutrition

progressivemedicalcenter.com

nccih.nih.gov/health/naturopathy

grounded.com

ncbi.nlm.nih.gov/pmc/articles/PMC4378297

washingtonpost.com/news/wonk/wp/2015/06/01/when-to-drink-coffee-so-you-get-the-most-out-of-the-caffeine

youtube.com/watch?v=IwAZn4O6sb4

`

Special Resource Section

"What Would Jesus Do?" from the ArchKennedy.com Blog

I want to start off by saying, what I am about to tell you is not out of vengeance. But I do feel that people need to hear my story, and I also hope that my words will help someone else who has suffered the same pain as I have. For the first time in my life, I was rejected from joining a church because I am gay. The particular church is The Church of The Apostles in Atlanta, Georgia.

Two months ago, I attended their "First Look" class, which is for those wanting to become members. After that, I scheduled my interview with one of the pastors on the next step to becoming a member. I was so excited because, after years of going to church here and there, I never wanted to be a part of a church community more than The Church of The Apostles. At this time in my life, I deeply need fellowship with other Christians. I have never felt like I belong anywhere. I don't fit into the gay world because I am a conservative. I don't fit into the straight world because I don't have a wife and kids. Becoming a member of this church would have really helped my self-esteem and made me feel part of a loving community. I have never needed it more than now.

I was doing men's Bible study, and the associate pastors were urging me to do a 26-week ministry called "Living Waters," which states:

> *"The discipleship and prayer ministry of Living Waters addresses the roots of relational and sexual issues that ensnare Christians into unhealthy living. Living Waters is about finding a way to admitting brokenness, and finally accepting the only way to wholeness is by discovering what the healing power of a relationship with Jesus really means."*

It sounded like a wonderful thing to me. I thought it would help me grow in my relationship with Christ and help me at least understand why I was gay. In hindsight, I now know that they wanted to "convert" me before granting me membership. Here's the thing. I have prayed for years not to be gay. I have spent many a day praying to God for me to be attracted to women. I still do this today. But, I could never promise a church that I will have an attraction to the opposite sex one day. All I know is that if you put a pretty woman and man in front of me, I will be attracted to the man. So because I say that I don't know if I could ever have opposite-sex attraction mean I don't have faith? I read Scripture daily in hopes of the answer someday. Until then, I have to be honest about who I am, and that should not deny me the chance to follow Christ with fellow believers.

I find Michael Youssef's sermons profound, and I love the fact that he does not "sugarcoat" the Scripture just to make people feel good. Dr. Youssef tells it like it is, and he is not afraid to lose members for preaching God's truth. I really admire that. So many churches today in an effort to keep and grow members, have become "social justice" churches and don't put Christ first and ignore what God is teaching us in Scripture. To me, that is very dangerous as we need to hear the Word even if it makes us uncomfortable. This allows us to repent and strive to be like Jesus. Sometimes the truth hurts, but I believe we must hear it for spiritual growth.

Those who know me know of my struggle with my faith and my sexuality. One thing I have said time and again is that I will NEVER try to change the Word of God just to suit my needs. I was honest about this struggle with the pastors at The Church of The Apostles. I could have possibly understood their not accepting me if I had told them that it is perfectly fine to be gay and that God has no problem with it. But, I never said that. I was just honest with my struggle. That being said, I believe that this church should reread Luke 15:1-7:

> "15 Now the tax collectors and sinners were all gathering around to hear Jesus. 2 But the Pharisees and the teachers of the law muttered, "This man welcomes sinners and eats with them.

> "3 Then Jesus told them this parable: 4 'Suppose one of you has a hundred sheep and loses one of them. Doesn't he leave the ninety-nine in the open country and go after the lost sheep until he finds it? 5 And when he finds it, he joyfully puts it on his shoulders 6 and goes home.' "Then he calls his friends and neighbors together and says, 'Rejoice with me; I have found my lost sheep.' 7 I tell you that in the same way there will be more rejoicing in heaven over one sinner who repents than over ninety-nine righteous persons who do not need to repent."

Now I ask you, if Jesus can do this, should not the church also? I think the answer is a resounding YES. Churches should never reject a person who wants to follow Jesus Christ. Never. Maybe the pastors at The Church of The Apostles forgot this verse. Or maybe, just maybe... they are imperfect sinners just like me.

Acknowledgments

First, I would first like to thank my partner in life and confidant, Leon Morales. Without his love and support during the darkest decade of my life, I am sure I would not be alive today. Leon stood by me and believed in me when I did not believe in myself and was literally at the end of my rope. For that, I am forever grateful.

Second, I also want to express my immense gratitude to Kevin Light for his professional support and guidance in the writing of my first book. Without him, it could not have been done. Because of our similar backgrounds and worldviews, Kevin was a tremendous help in writing on some very tough and controversial subject matter.

Third, I would also like to thank my dear friend, Amber Goldberg. She loved me when I could not love myself and helped me to learn that life was worth living sober.

Finally, a huge thank you to Bridgette Anderson, Carol Pocklington, Todd Cosper, Bill Britt, Lucinda Dallas, Jim Glover, Russ Goins, Beth Snider, and Joe Stout for your valuable feedback before the book was published.

About the Author

Arch comes from a family of broadcasters, so it is no surprise that he ended up working for 17 years as a broadcast meteorologist. After receiving a Bachelor of Science in meteorology and a minor in mathematics from Florida State University, he began his career in Macon, Georgia, "paying his dues" in the industry.

Later, Arch was able to make the jump to the Atlanta market, where he enjoyed eight years working at several local affiliates, WXIA and WSB, and on networks such as The Weather Channel, CNN, and Headline News forecasting the weather for millions. His career then took him to WFTV in Orlando, Florida and finally to a chief job in Nashville, Tennessee, at WZTV.

A shift in his life occurred when he came back home to take care of his mother in her last three years of life. After his mother's passing, he has continued to apply his experience as a recovering alcoholic doing two years of heavy research on the addicted brain. His goal is now to speak and train others on overcoming their challenges and achieving a meaningful life filled with purpose.

Learn more about Arch and his work at ArchKennedy.com.

Inspirational Speaker and Storyteller

If you've connected with the experiences in this book and want to take the next step with Arch, there are a couple of in-person opportunities to hear more.

Invite Arch to speak at your event or gathering either as a keynote presenter or how to use and apply Scripture to face the real challenges of life. Share his stories and experiences with your audience, and identify the inspirational key points in Arch's methods for overcoming challenges that you'd like them to hear. Other speaking passions include addiction, politics, and health and nutrition.

Learn More at ArchKennedy.com